March 2012

Engaging Mission:
the lasting value of Industrial
Mission for today

by

Peter Cope and Mike West

**Grosvenor House
Publishing Limited**

This book is published by
Grosvenor House Publishing Ltd
28-30 High Street, Guildford, Surrey, GU1 3EL.
www.grosvenorhousepublishing.co.uk

A CIP record for this book
is available from the British Library

ISBN 978-1-908596-81-9

31 employee involvmt - W. Temple
F D Maurice
34 uncle eric

Contents

Foreword by the Rt Revd Michael Bourke   v

Photographs   ix

Abbreviations used in the text   xi

Introduction   xiii

Chapter 1: The Story of Industrial Mission in Britain   1

An overview from beginnings in the19[th] century and early 20th century, early work in Sheffield, South London; the break-up of the Sheffield team in 1965; the Industrial Mission Association; economic and political changes of the 1980s; changed church priorities in the 1990s and at the end of the millennium.

Chapter 2: The Original Theology of Industrial Mission   29

The missiological context of early IM and the influences on L S Hunter and E R Wickham; the influence of F D Maurice, Richard and Reinhold Niebuhr, Paul Tillich and Dietrich Bonhoeffer; perceiving God's actions; understanding and living the Gospel.

Chapter 3: Theological and Ethical Development Within Industrial Mission   46

Creating an inductive theology; the work of David Jenkins and Ian Fraser; the Hermeneutical Cycle, the Theological Grid and the Flying Machine; the development of Christian ethics; the work of the Theology Development Group.

Photographs 71

Chapter 4: The Method of Mission in the Workplace 77

The development of the Sheffield and South London models of workplace chaplaincy; strategic priorities in developing workplace chaplaincy; diversification beyond large heavy manufacturing into small companies, science parks, the retail sector, local authorities, emergency services, etc; negotiating a new workplace chaplaincy; strategy in industrial disputes and plant closures.

Chapter 5: Mission Beyond the Workplace 104

The Homeworking Project; national networks in large national industries and around common concerns; European contacts and projects; the concern for South Africa; Corporate Social Responsibility.

Chapter 6: Industrial Mission and the Churches 125

Involvement in congregational activities and structures; lay training and formation; programmes for pre- and post-ordination training.

Chapter 7: The Living Legacy of Industrial Mission 135

Mission in society; early 21st century is not so different from that in heavy industry in the 1940s and 50s; the need for a Kingdom Theology; understanding the secular world and developing a contextual theology; the ministry of lay people; the task of the church as public institution; training and resourcing of ministers and church leaders.

So what is the legacy of IM?

Bibliography 154

Index 165

FOREWORD

Rt Revd Michael Bourke

The parallels between Industrial Mission (IM) in Britain and the Priest-Worker movement in France are instructive. Both began in the Second World War: the Priest-Workers launched their campaign in response to the Catholic Church's radical report *France, Pays de Mission*, and Industrial Mission arose from a similar assessment (voiced by Bishop Leslie Hunter) that 'England is once again a mission field'. And on the threshold of Germany's defeat Dietrich Bonhoeffer addressed the same missiological question: 'People as they are now simply cannot be religious any more. How can Christ become the Lord of the religionless as well?'

Peter Cope and Mike West have done us a good service in tracing the major contribution which IM has made, along with partners like the Iona Community, in bringing social justice into the forefront of the Church's mission. *Engaging Mission* is historically illuminating, and is the product of the authors' lifelong commitment to IM as well as of good research. It acknowledges candidly the limitations, setbacks and unresolved challenges as well as recording IM's numerous achievements. Among many good things it reminds us of IM's abiding ecumenical commitment, its involvement in the Lucas Aerospace Shop Stewards' 'Alternative Strategy', its pioneering role in Anglo-German trade union contacts at Vauxhall-Opel, its Europe-wide support of Homeworkers, its influence on training and work creation schemes for unemployed people, and its courses and placements for pre-ordination students.

The agenda of IM has been both ambitious and ambiguous. One of its original purposes was to bridge the gulf of alienation between the Churches and working class people, especially men, within heavy industry. The other was to forge a new theological understanding of the way in which the economic and technical forces of industry shape people's lives, and to bring Christian influence to bear on these structures. The two aims could be held together, but in practice they have generated tension over the meaning of 'mission'. The regular visiting of factories by industrial chaplains was intended by Leslie Hunter to promote 'a better quality of evangelism', and their input into factory discussions and training led to hopes, if not of a revival of congregational life, then at least of 'fresh expressions' of church. But the evangelistic motive was played down by the majority of Industrial Missioners, who like Ted Wickham gave priority to the theological and structural agenda. This has not always made it easy for IM to relate to the life of the various denominations, or to their strong evangelical constituencies.

Two major developments have changed the context in which IM works. One is the wholesale dismantling of the heavy industrial base carried out by the Thatcher Governments, which reinforced the affluent majority's self-perception as 'consumers' rather than as 'worker/producers'. So comprehensive was this change that IM, like the Church generally, was unsure how to respond: should its chaplains fight closures tooth and nail, or transfer to the new world of shopping malls, small businesses, airports and ethical investment? Should IM oppose the destruction of the old male-dominated culture and work-ethic of traditional industrial communities, or embrace the new opportunities of gender-equality? Having tried rather unsuccessfully to chair the Church of England's Industrial and Economic Affairs Committee in the early 1990s (with which IM was affiliated), I know how we failed to offer, in the British context, the kind of sustained critique of the strident half-truths of the free-market ideologues which the German Protestants achieved so competently in their 1992 Report *Common Good and Self-Interest*.

The most influential response to the Thatcher era was of course *Faith in the City*, which received a remarkably wide degree of support from both within and beyond the Churches. But its strategy of tackling structural injustices through projects based in communities and parishes may also have contributed to the marginalisation of IM. It was always true that parishes could, like IM, have a commitment to justice and an inductive approach to theology – witness Alan Ecclestone's parish meetings at Darnall in Hunter's Sheffield. But *Faith in the City* made parish-based action much more mainstream, and IM could no longer claim to be a lone voice for structural change in an individualistic church. It is one thing for

Industrial Missioners to welcome parish clergy and archdeacons as colleagues on regeneration programmes, and another for them to wonder precisely what their own distinctive role and contribution may now be.

The current climate of theological conservatism, financial constraint and structural adventurousness in the churches creates both difficulties and opportunities for IM. Money for chaplaincies is harder to argue for, and this is leading to parish-based IM appointments and to seeking funds from industries themselves. IM teams up and down the country are innovating to implant work-based ministry within the DNA of parishes themselves, by encouraging parish ministers to visit workplaces and undertake work-shadowing, and by providing resources for worship, teaching and training. IM's original purpose of infiltrating the world of work is as important as ever. The context may have changed from smokestack industries employing thousands of men in organised trades unions to self-employed individuals in small businesses, people trying to hold together a portfolio of short-term contracts, and insecure and low-paid employment in call-centres and care homes. But their stories still need to be heard, shared and honoured within the church's life of prayer and reflection.

Three particular conversations need to accompany IM's ongoing vocation. The first is with evangelical initiatives such as Mark Greene's work at the London Institute for Contemporary Christianity. This is briefly mentioned in Chapter 7, but a fuller critical dialogue is needed. It is striking that, despite its commitment to developing discipleship at work, there is no reference in the London Institute's literature to the long experience, vocation and wisdom of IM in this area. If there is a mutual nervousness it needs to be addressed.

The second conversation must be theological. The impulse behind the French Priest-Worker movement lay in Catholic incarnational theology combined with the tradition of celibacy: a priest could be called to fulfil his vocation as *alter Christus* by sharing the insecurity and poverty of workers – a radically different approach to that of factory visiting. And the theological roots of Bonhoeffer's 'religionless Christianity' lay in the Lutheran understanding of Justification as much as in sociological analysis. These theological foundations have not always been well understood in the more empirical culture of Anglo-Saxon countries, where 'the Kingdom of God' has represented the default position of IM, as these pages attest. The theology of the Kingdom of God has served us well in focussing attention on *the world* and not just *the church*, and on God's purpose for *collective life in this world* as well as for *individual salvation in the next world*. But IM has not always noted the tension between the Kingdom of God as a present reality – something we can 'build' – and as an eschatological hope – something that cannot be achieved by human effort, but only awaited from God. The Anglo-Saxon preference for the former created an optimism which unravelled as the post-war consensus was dismantled, and it is interesting that *Engaging Mission* concludes with a much more eschatological meditation on the Kingdom of God rooted in another tradition. At the very least, a new ecumenical conversation about the theology of Industrial Mission now needs to take place on a Europe-wide basis.

The third conversation is about spirituality. IM has done good work on providing liturgical and intercessory material for congregations, but less on spiritual direction for people in their working lives. How can people be helped to understand their situation and the forces which shape it? Tell their stories? Pray through the crises, difficulties and temptations? Resist pressure and propaganda? Make responsible decisions? Take responsibility with and for others, and change things for the better? Celebrate achievement and good fortune? Handle prosperity or poverty? And remain human? Such concerns were close to the surface in the schooling undertaken in the early days of the Sheffield IM, and the present interest in discipleship suggests that this conversation should be revitalised.

We are indebted to Mike West and Peter Cope for providing us with such a valuable resource to understand the past, and prepare for the next stage of IM's contribution to the overall mission of the Church.

Michael Bourke, Bishop of Wolverhampton 1993-2006

Photographs

Photo 1
Ted Wickham in Firth Vickers Steels, Sheffield, mid-1950s.

Photo 2
Margaret Kane in Firth Brown Special Steel works, Sheffield, circa 1962.

Photo 3
Mike West in Hawker Siddeley Aviation, Hatfield, June 1977.

Photo 4
Peter Cope in Brockhouse Forgings Ltd, West Bromwich, 1993.

Photo 5
Lyn Jamieson with Turgut Turna, owner of Demure in MetroCentre, Gateshead, 2002.

Photo 6
Andrew Jolly on the Total Manifold Compression Platform 173 Km north of Aberdeen. Andrew was awarded the MBE for his work in 2009 and sadly died in 2010.

Photo 7
Mike Fox at GKN Land Systems,28 April 2011, with two shop stewards, planting a tree to mark Workers' Memorial Day.

Photo 8
Opel Trades Unionists visiting Vauxhall Motors, Luton, September 1974.

Photo 9
Yorkshire and Portuguese Homeworkers during a conference in Leeds brought together by the West Yorkshire Homeworkers Group 1991. Dian Leppington third from right.

Photo 10
Sheffield Industrial Mission Theological Students Summer School – visiting Thurnscoe Colliery, June 1987.

Photo 11
Industrial Mission Association Induction Course; Training visit to Vauxhall Motors, January 1999.

Photo 12
Redundancy – The Last Option, booklet published by Newport and Gwent Industrial Mission, 1979.

We are grateful to the following for granting permission to use these photographs:

1	Jenny Wickham for the photo of her father.
2 and 10	Workplace Chaplaincy South Yorkshire, formerly Industrial Mission in South Yorkshire and Sheffield Industrial Mission.
5	Lyn Jamieson
6	UK Oil and Gas Chaplaincy for the photo of Andrew Jolly.
7	Black Country Urban and Industrial Mission
9	Dian Leppington.

The other photographs are the property of the authors.

Abbreviations used in the text

BSR   Board for Social Responsibility of General Synod. Its Industrial (later Industrial and Economic Affairs) Committee included two representatives of the Industrial Mission Association.

CCIM   Churches' Consortium on Industrial Mission; a working party composed of the churches' national officers concerned for Industrial Mission and representatives of the IMA. Established under the British Council of Churches in 1975 and succeeded by Industrial and Economic Mission (INDEM) in 1990 when the BCC was replaced by Churches Together in Britain and Ireland (CTBI). INDEM operates largely as an electronic network sharing common issues and interests between denominations and those engaged in workplace chaplaincy and faith-work projects.

ECG   European Contact Group for Church and Industry (from 1965 to 1987) and for Urban Industrial Mission (after 1987). The European Regional Group under the auspices of the Urban and Industrial Mission (later Urban Rural Mission) desk of the Commission on World Mission and Evangelism (CWME) of the World Council of Churches. Usually two British delegates, one nominated by the CCIM and one by IMA.

GS   General Synod of the Church of England.

ICF   Industrial Christian Fellowship; created in 1919 by the amalgamation of the Navvy Mission and the Christian Social Union.

IM   Industrial Mission, either as the generally accepted name for the movement, or in the title of specific teams.

IMA   Industrial Mission Association; the membership organisation founded in 1969 for those engaged in IM.

INDEM   Industrial and Economic Mission working party. An informal group 'in association with CTBI'.

TDG   Theology Development Group of the IMA.

Introduction

In the second half of the twentieth century the churches in Britain began a serious engagement with industrial people and organisations, employing the largest single group of clergy and ministers outside the parochial ministry. This was possible at a time when church resources of money and staff were more plentiful than in later years. It took advantage of the post war spirit of the times within industry and in the wider society. It drew on a set of protestant theologies which were particularly appropriate for those years. For most of that period it was known as Industrial Mission (IM). Had the term been available IM might claim to be the *first* 'fresh expression' of church! This book springs directly from our experience; we have both played a part in the rise and expansion of Industrial Mission as a movement in the British churches, and been involved in its decline.

This book tells the story of the theology and the strategies of IM teams around Britain over 65 years as a key example of Christian mission in the twentieth century. We hope that the experience of IM can help to fashion an appropriate mission in the twenty-first century.

Christian mission gives expression to the dynamic relationship between God and the world, particularly as this was portrayed in … Jesus of Nazareth.(1)

It is about sharing in the life of God the Trinity, a sharing which humans experience as love, justice, truth and goodness. Mission is a movement from God to the world in which the church is an instrument. Indeed, this movement is the prime reason for the church's existence. 'There is church because there is mission, not vice versa.' (2)

In the latter years of the twentieth century the competition for the diminishing resources and rising costs of the churches led to the decline in the support for IM and a sharper focus on congregations and their existing members. The growing popularity of other theologies and strategies of mission also played a part in the decline. We have personal experience of the shrinking of IM – one of us was made redundant, and the other's post was discontinued on his retirement.

Having both worked in Industrial Mission in different areas of Britain for nearly 40 years, and having had this opportunity to reflect, we are well aware of the inadequacies and weaknesses of IM. The movement began as a partnership for ordained and lay Christians committed to make clear God's presence and purposes within industrial society. This largely failed to take root and the work became professionalized, even clericalised. Lay people had an important role in the leadership of the work in Sheffield, but elsewhere where there were lay groups, they took on an educational rather than mission role. The creative national organisation (the Industrial Mission Association) which played such a key role in developing the work became in effect a professional association for industrial chaplains.

Early work in Sheffield had an explicit as well as an implicit missionary (and even evangelistic) purpose. At its height IM claimed that it 'works for the reordering of the relationships, methods and goals of industry and commerce in the light of the Christian hope for justice and community'. (3) In the changing climate towards the end of the century these hopes declined and much IM work became mainly pastoral in character, and was deliberately rebranded as Workplace Chaplaincy. Chaplains wanted to raise important prophetic questions with people at different levels of companies, but inevitably often found that the need to remain in that situation compelled compromises. Nevertheless, in spite of these failures, we remain convinced that IM embodied key features of an appropriate mission for modern society.

The priority of mission in the church's life – mission in the broadest sense of enabling the lives of individuals and the structures of society to be transformed by God's Kingdom of love and justice – has sometimes led IM into conflict with the institutional church, and perhaps contributed to its decline. This book is about those who have been caught by the vision that people and communities can be transformed by God's coming Kingdom – not only industrial chaplains but many lay people who would not call themselves church members. They can be reassured that the value of the work is publicly acknowledged by the church. As the carefully researched and written report *Industrial Mission – an Appraisal* declares:

> *IM is ... the focus of intense concern about the nature of Christian witness in today's world ... It has been from its beginning, therefore, an extended seminar in applied theology ... In the process of clarifying its own mission, [IM] has raised issues about the mission of the whole church in the world.* (4)

When we began researching and writing this book in November 2007 there were only a handful of serious studies of IM and none published since 2000. Since then *Bridgebuilders: Workplace chaplaincy – a history* has appeared, written by our friend and colleague Malcolm Torry. (5) We are very grateful to Malcolm for the wealth of background material on the beginnings of IM in both Sheffield and South London which he has included, and to which we have made reference. However, Malcolm himself has acknowledged that his work deals exclusively with workplace chaplaincy activities within industrial mission, and only touches on theological issues relevant to these activities. Our work obviously has a much broader focus. Malcolm also constructs his book around a particular view of secularisation which we do not find convincing or completely consistent. Secularisation is indeed a major issue for the churches, but not necessarily hostile to the gospel or the Kingdom.

We would like to acknowledge the help which many people have given us in the task of writing this book, especially Revd Canon Dr John Atherton, Revd Rod Garner, Professor Elaine Graham - and Revd Dr Crispin and Mrs Mary White for their efforts in proof-reading. We are indebted to Rachel Britton for her excellent design for the front cover (from an idea by Mike West) We are also very grateful for the financial support of the Industrial Mission Association, without which publication would not have been possible. We would also like to pay tribute very much to our respective spouses – Melia and Pam – for their patience and support in the time and effort required to produce a volume like this.

Peter Cope Mike West September 2011

Notes and references to the Introduction

1 *Transforming Mission,* David J Bosch, Orbis Books (1991) p 8.
2 Aagard, quoted by Bosch, reference above, p 390.
3 From *Guidelines on the Task, Organisation, Appointments and Continuity of Industrial Mission* Churches Consortium on Industrial Mission, quoted in *Industrial Mission – an Appraisal* Church of England Board for Social Responsibility (1988) p xiii.
4 *Industrial Mission – an Appraisal,* p 49.
5 Published by Canterbury Press, 2010.

Dedication

To all our brothers and sisters in Industrial Mission, and to the men and women who have shared their lives with us in countless workplaces and taught us so much about the nature of God's Kingdom

CHAPTER ONE

The Story of Industrial Mission in Britain

We are living in an industrial community while thinking and talking as though we were still in a pre-industrial society. The lack of contact between the industrial worker, whether of the management or of the managed, and the parochial life of the church is very serious. The two worlds hardly touch. We seem to him strange to the world of his livelihood and life.

Leslie Hunter, Bishop of Sheffield in *Let us go Forward*, May 1944.

This chapter tells the story of Industrial Mission, or at least enough of it to support the subsequent chapters. Some particular elements of the history are set out in more detail in those chapters. Although the movement already had a history and a tradition our focus begins in 1944 with the appointment of E R (Ted) Wickham as an Industrial Chaplain in Sheffield. It finishes with a sketch of the movement at the end of that millennium.

Origins

For more than 100 years the churches had recognised that in the burgeoning industrial cities their congregations included a small proportion of 'working men'. Before the end of the nineteenth century it was being said that 'The Church of England has not lost the working class, she never had them'. (1) In most of those cities there were imaginative attempts to recruit working men through brighter services and less forbidding buildings, but the problem remained. The Navvy Mission was founded in 1877 as an evangelistic movement to the railway constructers in their out of town encampments. Lay ministers were appointed to visit their camps, to hold services and undertake pastoral work. The Visitors soon found that there were particular pastoral problems arising out of the navvies' employment which they sought to alleviate, and to

1

campaign for their abolition. In 1920 the Navvy Mission amalgamated with the intellectual Christian Social Union to form the Industrial Christian Fellowship (ICF). In their 'front line battle to convert industrial Britain' the ICF employed a number of lay Missioners who visited factories. The experience of Army Chaplains during the First World War showed them how little working class men were involved with the life of mainstream protestant churches. Of course Anglican clergy in towns and cities would have called in to workplaces of all kinds as part of their normal parochial work.

Those visits were stepped up during the special industrial conditions of the Second World War, when men and women were directed to work away from home and many more women were engaged in production. Cuthbert Bardsley, Vicar of Woolwich made contact with the employees of Siemens Brothers in the air-raid shelters they used. He established a Quiet Room in the factory, and in 1942 regular lunch-time services began. Colin Cuttell extended this work, which became organized as South London Industrial Mission (SLIM) in 1952. Torry comments: 'Bardsley saw the task in the same way that armed forces chaplains saw theirs: visiting the sick, keeping men in touch with their families when they were at work during air raids, and conducting services.' He adopted the title of 'padre'. The early SLIM chaplains all modelled their work on Cuttell. 'Some of the clergy saw their factory visiting as simply normal parish visiting, and those who were visiting sites not in their parishes still saw themselves as parish priests doing parish visiting'. (2) This aspect of IM work was given lower priority by full time chaplains in later years, only re-emerging as more and more work was undertaken by part-time volunteers.

There were special opportunities in the Shadow factories set up in rural areas to make munitions. Wickham was full-time chaplain to the Swynnerton Explosives factory in Staffordshire from 1941 – 44. The work in Scotland began in 1941 when Ian Fraser was appointed by the Church of Scotland Home Board with a similar brief to Wickham's. (3)

These projects by the church to reach industrial workers in their places of work are one strand of the history of Industrial Mission. The second and increasingly the more important strand was the Christian Social Tradition. This had been growing since the middle of the nineteenth century. Many anglo-catholic priests working in slum parishes, nonconformists running inner city missions and students volunteering in University Settlements had all been radicalised by their experiences. At first only a few radicals called themselves Christian Socialists. They never had a major effect on congregations but in the early decades of the twentieth century it was said that amongst Bishops and academics most were known to be supporters of the Labour Party if not full members. In 1919 the Archbishop's Commission on Christianity and Industrial Problems concluded (with substantial caveats) that: 'in certain fundamental respects the existing industrial system itself is gravely defective'. (4) In the inter war years these ideas were formulated and studied in a series of major conferences, notably the Conference on Christian Politics, Economics and Citizenship (COPEC) held in Birmingham in 1924. At this stage we should notice that most of those appointed as Industrial Chaplains in the early decades were committed to Social Christianity more strongly than most of their fellow clergy, and sought to bring it to bear in their industrial visiting. There was a pink tinge to Industrial Mission from its beginning.

If Wickham was the key pioneer of IM then Bishop Leslie Hunter was the movement's Godfather. In the 1930s he had been directly involved in many of the meetings which had focussed the Christian Social Tradition. (cf *Strategist for the Spirit*) (5). When he became Bishop of Sheffield in 1939 he was dismayed by the gulf between the Diocese and the great mass of workers in the steel industry which dominated the area. In1944 he appointed Wickham, at first half-time, to be an 'Industrial Padre'. As well as taking a close interest in the experiment as it developed, he also wrote perceptively of the need to embody Christianity in the heart of the new industrial culture, or else 'a bleak, amoral superficial secularism would thrive'. (6)

One key milestone in IM's move from experiment to pilot stage occurred in 1949. Bishop Hunter reviewed the work in Sheffield, and resolved that it should be 'urgently expanded'. (7) As a result Wickham was moved from his part-time post as Chaplain to the Shrewsbury Hospital (Almshouses for elderly people) to become a Canon Residentiary of Sheffield Cathedral. Leslie Hayes joined Wickham in 1948, creating the first team of full-time chaplains. The team grew and by 1960 Sheffield Industrial Mission (SIM) had a full-time staff of eight, including two women chaplains, Kay Hancock from 1953 and Margaret Kane from 1959.

Early growth

During the 1950s many Dioceses covering major industrial areas appointed Industrial Chaplains, some using the Sheffield model and others with parish based work like that of SLIM. In Bristol (John Ragg) and Birmingham (Ralph Stevens) city centre churches were designated as centres to help other churches develop relationships with local factories, which did not necessarily involve workplace chaplaincy. In Luton there were two initiatives, one begun in 1954 based on the Methodist Chapel Street chapel (Bill Gowland), and the other in 1955 based on the Anglican parish of Christ Church (Maurice Jenkins). Both were launched with an explicit evangelistic emphasis; one of the industrialists supporting Jenkins wrote of his hope that 'in five years we expect to see a steady flow of newly converted workers into our parish churches'. This common aim did not create collaboration and when in 1956 the Methodist Chapel was renamed 'Luton Industrial Mission' there was talk of legal action by the Anglicans. (8)

There were several features in the 'Sheffield model' which became normative as the work spread to other industrial areas. Its foundation was establishing contacts at all level in workplaces of dominant industries, together with city or regional contacts with management organisations and trades unions. Groups were gathered together in work places (where that was possible) and after work to discuss the potential connections between Christian faith and the industrial world. The key members of these groups would be developed through day and residential conferences. Whether these activities would lead to people seeking membership of their local churches, or establishing new para-church congregations was an issue between the early practitioners.

IM enters the mainstream

In the late 1950s three publications brought IM to the attention of a wider public, not only those within the church. The first was Wickham's book about Sheffield, *Church and People in an Industrial City*. (9) It was widely welcomed as the first major study of the responses by the churches to industrialisation. In its last chapter, *The Mission of the Church in an Industrial Society*, he sets out his

4

theology and strategy. Here was an understanding of mission which was far wider than evangelism or church growth, but which some critics failed to appreciate.

In 1959 the Church Assembly (the predecessor of the Church of England's General Synod) debated a major report *The Task of the Church in Relation to Industry* and accepted most of its recommendations. (10) Wickham was the Committee's Secretary. It brought IM to the attention of a wider Church of England audience and could be said to be the point at which IM became firmly established in the mainstream of church life.

It argued that the Church's Concern for Industry could be based on this syllogism (sic):

> *The Christian church is concerned with the quality of human life, both of men individually and of their society.*

> *Industry, the industrial organisation of society determines to a very large degree the quality of human life, both of men and of their society.*

> *Therefore the Church should be concerned with industry and the industrial organisation of society.*

For many chaplains this became their text when asked 'what have you come to do?'

The report contained 11 pages outlining the current work programme of the five longest-established teams (Sheffield, SLIM, Bristol, Birmingham, Coventry) with further reference to five others which had recently started (Liverpool, East London, Manchester, Reading, and Rochester). The list of activities was heavily weighted towards the Sheffield example and may have been less representative of some other teams. The headings were:

- Regular visiting the basic industry and larger works of the area.
- The organization of informal groups of men. (sic)
- Representing a point of view within the councils of the Church, including clergy training.
- Training of laymen in industry.

The Committee's recommendations covered four aspects:

- Laity should be encouraged to become involved as part of their Christian duty in politics, professional organisations and Trades Unions.
- A recognition that the Parish Clergy, 'the normal missionary and parochial structure of the Church's life could not grapple with the totality of this task'.
- IM must be maintained at a high level of competence and quality.
- Need for a National Industrial Secretariat, to oversee the work and develop national contacts.

The Church Assembly generally approved the recommendations and instructed the Central Board of Finance to prepare a money resolution. The Industrial Committee when it was formed appointed John Rogan an ex-Sheffield Chaplain as its Secretary. He and his successors were never given the resources or the authority for the complete range of those tasks. The preparation and publication of the Committee's reports into industrial issues was the most visible and in may ways useful aspect of their work. (11) The Industrial Mission Association (IMA) founded in 1969 took up the first three areas and made considerable progress in them.

The third publication was *Christians in an Industrial Society* written by Richard Taylor, a Congregational Minister about to become an industrial chaplain. (12) He writes that the work is 'still at a highly experimental stage'. He took a wider view of the work on the ground, outlining the established work in Sheffield, South London, Bristol and Birmingham and newer teams in Warrington, Scunthorpe, Rochester, Crawley, Coventry, Port Talbot and Stockton.

As well as the influence of Wickham's writing and speaking there were organisational reasons for the emergence of Sheffield as the normative model. From 1950 SIM held annual conferences for ordinands, in which many caught the IM virus and sooner or later sought to become Industrial Chaplains. Michael Jackson (who joined the SIM staff in 1953, and was Senior Chaplain 1960 – 69); Philip Bloy (SIM staff 1952 – 62) and Bill Wright (seconded to SIM for 4 years before starting the work in Stockton-on-Tees); Simon Phipps (Coventry Industrial Mission) and Michael Atkinson (SIM

1957 -66, then Northampton 1966 – 71 and Croydon 1971 – 75) came in later years.

At the same time a major innovation in clergy training was established. Ordinands came to Sheffield for a year, worked as unskilled labourers in steel works, lodged with local families and shared in the group work of the Mission. (see Chapter 6) Between 1950 and 1966, 200 men took part in the scheme, including Bill Dudman and Peter Challen who spent most of their ministries in IM. Nowhere else had this investment in clergy training which helped to spread the Sheffield model throughout Britain. Some new Missions, like Teesside sent their newly appointed chaplains to Sheffield for shorter periods to learn the craft. Ironically when the first full-time post was created in evangelically oriented Luton, it was a Sheffield part-time chaplain, Ivor Clemitson, who was appointed and re-shaped the work on the Sheffield model.

Throughout the 1960s the number of full-time posts increased and teams were established in new areas. However the proposal to establish a powerful national Industrial Secretariat in which it was assumed that Wickham would be the national organiser of IM was watered down. IM would remain under the control of Diocesan Bishops, with all the variability that entailed.

The Sheffield Crisis
In 1966 IM came to the attention of a wider audience because of the crisis within the founding team Sheffield. Editorials in *The Times* (21 June 1966) and *The Guardian* (23 July 1966) ensured that people not normally interested in church affairs were informed. Bagshaw has many of the details; here it is necessary to give the outline in order to explain later events. (13)

Wickham was not given the national post and was persuaded to accept consecration as the Suffragan Bishop of Middleton in November 1959. He was replaced as Senior Chaplain by Michael Jackson, who had been a member of the team since 1953. Bishop Hunter began to press him for some results in the anticipated recruitment of new church members from within the Mission's lay membership. When Hunter was succeeded in 1962 by an evangelical bishop, John Taylor, the tension between the traditional church and IM became more evident. The Mission's work continued largely unchanged, although in the changing industrial climate the content of lay groups shifted from religious to industrial topics. At the same time Mission staff were influenced by theological trends, which gained notoriety in 1963 with the publication of John Robinson's *Honest to God* in which he praises Wickham for working at the relationship between theology and the real world. (14)

In 1965 Jackson sharply changed his theological position. He formed the opinion that some if not all of the staff were theologically and politically too radical for their task. He sacked two members of the team and in 1966 asked two more to leave. This was vigorously opposed by the chaplains, most of the lay groups and Sheffield trades unions. Jackson was supported by Bishop Taylor, who set out his position in a statement: 'The business of the Church, or any agency of the Church like Industrial Mission, is the making and nurturing of Christians'. (15)

Of the ten staff in post at the end of 1965 only two remained by January 1967. The sacked chaplains included the two nonconformist ministers, both without consultation with their denomination. The assumption that Industrial Mission had to be ecumenical ('industry would not tolerate any other model') had been formalised in 1958 in the British Council of Churches (BCC) document *Church and Industry*. (16) Ecumenical relations at the national level were set back for a decade. However this *diaspora* of Sheffield-trained chaplains to new posts further strengthened the influence of the (original) Sheffield model. Jackson soon moved to become Vicar of Doncaster, and it was more than ten years before Sheffield Industrial Mission re-entered the mainstream of Industrial Mission.

Chaplains across the country expressed their support for the Sheffield team. The crisis focussed attention on IM's dependence on episcopal support, which could be reduced or even withdrawn when a new Bishop was appointed. Informal national meetings of chaplains drew up plans which in 1969 resulted in the creation of the Industrial Mission Association (IMA). This voluntary organisation soon became the means through which chaplains cooperated nationally in relation to both industrial and church bodies. In 1979, in collaboration with the William Temple Foundation, it established and staffed the Induction Course, a further means of consolidating the mainstream model of IM, though no longer the Sheffield model.

In the changed industrial climate of the late 1960s IM teams became more engaged in debating key industrial issues. The Labour Government 1964 – 70 published *In Place of Strife* and the Report of the Royal Commission on Trades Unions and Employers' Associations (Donovan) in 1968. These were received favourably by chaplains. In 1970 the Revd Lord Peter Sandford, a junior Minister in the Conservative Government, consulted a group of chaplains about the proposals which became the Industrial Relations Act 1971. He was horrified to hear of their almost total opposition.

IM comes of age and develops new activities

In 1971 Trevor Beeson wrote in the *Christian Century* 'Industrial Mission has come of age'. Also in that year Archbishop Michael Ramsey addressed the first national conference of the IMA and urged those present 'to clamour for more resources'. Perhaps he had been particularly impressed by the Association's theological work, including the inductive model which only later would be labelled 'Doing Theology'. (see Chapter 3) Relations with the churches nationally were strengthened when the Church of England Industrial Committee invited the IMA to nominate two representatives, whilst the BCC Industrial Advisory Committee co-opted five chaplains. In 1972 that body established the Churches Consortium on Industrial Mission (CCIM), comprising the denominations' national officers concerned for IM and the IMA officers. For the first time the Conference of Roman Catholic Bishops was represented, although few priests were seconded to IM teams. The IMA grew from 120 to 140 full-time and many half- and part-time members, most of the increase by existing teams gaining more staff. There were discussions about the difficulty of recruiting suitable new staff, although there had been some improvement in the mobility of experienced chaplains. During the decade In-Service Theological Training courses leading to masters degrees were established at Hull and Cardiff Universities.

By now workplace chaplaincy had become not only the basic model, but was expected and welcomed in a wide variety of workplaces. Some teams were moving away from the earlier concentration on basic heavy industries with work amongst small firms (Teesside) and with local authorities. Unemployment had begun to be a concern, both in conferences and study groups and in 1972 a full-time specialist was appointed in Lincoln. The Newport and Gwent team, noticing the lack of support for people losing their jobs, published *Redundant - a survival kit*. Five teams used it the basis for short leaflets which were produced in large numbers and were often purchased by companies who were making employees redundant. In 1973 the Bristol team moved well beyond workplace chaplaincy when they held a public enquiry into the proposed closure and large scale redundancy at the Royal Naval base at Copenacre.

The regional and national structures of the IMA facilitated cooperation between chaplains engaged in the same company or industry. (see Chapter 5) Wickham had pointed to the need for this outside the parish structure of the Church of England in *Church and People in an Industrial City*. (17) Steel chaplains had been holding annual meetings since the early 60s, and held regular meetings with senior managers of the British Steel Corporation. In 1971 thirteen chaplains working in different parts of British Rail (BR) formed a network and by 1978 reported regular meetings with BR Directors, and national officers of the railway unions. Teams affected by large scale redundancies studied the Government's report into schemes for training unemployed people (the Holland Report) and arranged meetings with the Chairman and senior staff of the Manpower Services Commission (MSC). At one point the MSC asked the IMA to suggest members of District Manpower Boards, and many were appointed. By contrast an earlier invitation from the Department of Employment for chaplains to join the Industrial Tribunals set up under the Industrial Relations Act 1971 was energetically turned down. An article by Bill Wright of Teesside Industrial Mission on the effects of investment policies as seen from the local perspective led to an invitation from the Church Commissioners to a series of discussions with IMA representatives.

The potential for these networks of chaplains to lead to relationships with the head offices of companies, trades unions and government departments came to be called National Industrial Mission. From 1980 the IMA allocated some of its funds to resource these networks. They drew upon the strong sense of common identity amongst chaplains. One of the tasks of the Secretary of the Church

England Industrial Committee was to facilitate relationships with head offices of national companies and with government.

As the IMA enabled the creation of national networks, the European Contact Group for Urban Industrial Mission (ECG) helped British IM teams to make contact with IM projects connected to common industries and companies in Western Europe. (see Chapter 5) In 1978 the ECG reported on 18 exchange programmes involving British workers and managers and European counterparts with overlapping interests. Teams recruited participants to the ECG's Five Nations Shop Stewards Conference held annually in Brussels. Greater Manchester IM worked with a German IM team to research and publish an in-depth study of Industrial Participation. The Hertfordshire and Bedfordshire team organised exchanges of trades unionists between General Motors' two European companies, Vauxhall and Opel. (see Chapter 5) This contributed to the formation of a General Motors Europe Trades Union Liaison group, a move which was not welcomed by the management!

One sign of IM's growing acceptance by the churches was teams' involvement in training. (see Chapter 6) Many teams were invited to lecture in Theological Colleges and provide student placements. However the year long industrial scheme for ordinands in Sheffield shrank as casual employment became harder to find, and stopped completely in 1980. Hertfordshire and Bedfordshire IM in collaboration with two local management training centres organised short courses for clergy and ministers on 'Understanding Industry'. As a contribution to the 1978 Lambeth Conference of Anglican Bishops IMA produced, a set of papers on Industrial Mission and held a conference with six overseas Bishops.

IM's external image continued to be the clergyman in a dirty and noisy workplace, and indeed this was still the majority of the work. But the changing economic situation was beginning to challenge the claim that the traditional neutral stance of the workplace chaplain could be combined with commitment to justice, peace and sustainability. Following an address by Management Consultant Dick Ottaway at the 1978 national conference Mostyn Davies regretted that industrial chaplains were not 'change agents they were researchers'. Another commented that 'there was plenty of analysis but little action'.

Perhaps the high point of the 1970s was CCIM document *Guidelines on the Task, Organisation, Appointments and Continuity of Industrial Mission* (18) which defined the task of IM:

a) IM is part of the whole mission of the church. It is concerned to further the purpose and work of God, as made known in Christ, within industry and industrial society, and to help the Church at large to see involvement in industrial and economic affairs as an essential part of its mission.

b) IM is a Christian activity which lay and ordained men and women share together. It involves taking part in the conversations which occur in the industrial world, being sensitive to what is happening and seeking to understand.

c) IM aims to discover the effect of industry on the people who work in it, the society which depends on it, and the world order which is being shaped by it.

d) IM works for the reordering of the relationships, methods and goals of industry and commerce, in the light of the Christian hope for justice and community, and through the process of participation, reflection and evaluation.

This document makes the grand claim that through the well established IM processes of 'participation, reflection and evaluation' IM could and indeed should, contribute to the 'reordering of the relationships, methods and goals of industry and commerce'.

Involvement in Issues and Problems

Industrial Mission had begun as an innovative missionary endeavour including the potential for creating new industrial para-church congregations. It was at home in the post war political consensus, and in many ways identified with that left of centre position. That consensus was about to be demolished by the Thatcher government.

As Britain moved from the Winter of Discontent in 1979 to the Conservative Government of Margaret Thatcher, with its clear commitment to a 'New Right' agenda it became clear that the social consensus of the 1950s and 60s had gone. This created a new agenda for IM with several divisive issues. The 1980 National Conference debated four key issues: Racial justice in Britain and

South Africa, Lucas Aerospace and other Worker Initiatives, and equality for women workers. Later the IMA would become committed to the World Council of Churches search for a 'Just, Participative and Sustainable Society' (JPSS) (19), though it was hard to find many specific or organised projects towards those goals. Julian Eagle based in Southampton was active in publicising the struggles of black workers and their trades unions in South Africa, and in particular urging that British companies with subsidiaries there should be challenged to sign up to the European Economic Communities' Code of Practice. He had some success in furthering this within the Transport and General Workers Union (TGWU), but not amongst the dock workers he met through his workplace chaplaincy. (see Chapter 5) Similarly in the North West Chris Percy's public involvement in racial justice issues undermined his acceptability with some local employers. On the other side Rodney Ward's chairmanship of a community-based MSC programme led to his expulsion from the Sunderland Trades Union Council. (20)

Some church agencies criticised IM's neutral stance, a feeling which grew after the publication of *Faith in the City* in 1985. (21) There was growing discussion within IM about the possibility of being both impartial and prophetic. The issue on which IM became very committed and involved was the rising tide of unemployment. In 1980 David Welbourn convened a major conference on 'The Impact of Unemployment on Norwich' and organised a support group for unemployed people. For a period members of the Scottish IM team mounted a presence at one unemployment benefit office. Many teams became involved in creating and in some cases managing government funded projects for unemployed people. In Grimsby a redundant church school become the St John's Centre teaching woodworking and other skills to both young people and adults. This experience was fed into annual National Industrial Mission meetings with senior management of the Manpower Services Commission, which in turn led to chaplains being co-opted to MSC regional advisory bodies. These issues were discussed in the Board for Social Responsibility of the General Synod of the Church of England (BSR) report *Work and the Future*. (22) A year later the IMA Theology Development Group (TDG) went further in *The End of Work*. (23)

IM national co-ordination was developing in several directions. The 1980 national conference had 140 participants and funds were set aside to meet some of the costs of National Industrial Mission. (see Chapter 5) The annual meeting of chaplains in the Central Electricity Generating Board (CEGB) was held in the CEGB staff college at the CEGB's expense. A method of theological reflection was developed in a series of training conferences provided by Ian Fraser at the Selly Oak Colleges, using Workers' Initiatives as case studies. Later it became known within IM as the Fraser method. (see Chapter 3) In 1981 the TDG met with a group of eight academic theologians who recommended that teams should establish contacts with theology departments in local universities. Teams were also urged to offer both placements and teaching to theological colleges.

In 1980 the IMA three-week Induction Course was launched, which was to become the central means of focussing and handing on IM's traditions and methods. At first it was a partnership between the IMA and William Temple Foundation, which already had training programmes for urban mission workers. Three five-day residential weeks were based in Manchester, using IM teams in the region in addition to two part-time Tutors. Later it became a wholly IMA venture, and moved location around Britain to make use of a wider range of IM teams. Almost all new full- and half-time chaplains participated and a growing number of part-time and voluntary chaplains. It is noteworthy that this was entirely staffed by IM staff seconded to the course, or (more accurately) who added this responsibility to their existing work load.

The year long dispute in the coal industry (March 1984 – March 1985) exposed IM's strengths and weaknesses at that time. The coal chaplains, through their strong national network with its links to the National Union of Mineworkers (NUM) at local and national level, were deeply involved in both the issues at stake and day to day events. Six national conferences drew in many other ministers in the coal fields, which produced briefing materials for church leaders of all denominations. The Home Counties North IMA Regional Group wrote to the Government urging a new, less aggressive approach to the dispute. Afterwards the BSR produced an 18-page report *The Church and the Miners' Strike.* (24) But within IM teams and throughout the movement there were those who, whilst concerned for the future of the coal communities, were critical of the NUM strategy. The IMA did not come to a position on the dispute and the pages of its monthly *Newsletter* scarcely mention the issue. Perhaps the vocal minority, focussed in the TDG Anti-Capitalist Group with its careful use of Marxist analysis, were running ahead of the majority.

In another area there was a well defined consensus on Government policy. With the rapid growth of unemployment the Government found the rising cost of its schemes harder to meet. One MSC official commented off the record in an annual meeting with IMA representatives that 'Government funding was overwhelmed by high unemployment', and that 'it was now impossible to fund good schemes'. Local churches, in many cases led by IM staff, were heavily involved in those programmes from the beginning. In South Yorkshire, an area hard hit by closures in the steel industry, half of all the MSC funded projects were church-based. As the schemes' funding regimes grew tighter it became almost impossible for the smaller community-based projects to continue. There was a debate with IM about the value of the schemes, dismissed by some as 'cosmetic'. By 1985 the consensus was for IM 'to get out of the Youth Training Scheme'.

A parallel argument was advocated by Antony Dalling a member of the Kent Industrial Mission team, a leader of the more radical wing. He had succeeded in launching two Unemployed People's Groups in his South London area, for campaigning and benefits advice. He urged other teams to follow his example, rather than continuing to support and even lead MSC projects. (25)

In the 1980s threats to IM staffing began to appear. Trevor Cooper had worked in Coventry IM for 13 years including leading their project for unemployed people, and managing an exchange programme for managers and trades unionists between Coventry and both East and West Germany. (see Chapter 5) He only narrowly avoided having his post terminated in 1982, but the threat did not go away. IM teams were urged to build new alliances with parishes around unemployment and third world trade issues.

Works' Chaplaincy is both affirmed and questioned
In 1982 the Churches' Consortium on Industrial Mission published *Starting the Work*, a compendium of advice based on over 35 years' experience of workplace chaplaincy. (26) It became the central document of the IMA Induction Training Course for a decade or

more. But the review in the *IMA Newsletter* by Ian Stubbs was very critical: 'It trains people to be like the best chaplains of the 60s and 70s' rather than for the future in which Stubbs predicted that 'Works Chaplaincy will soon be a minor activity'. (27) Many correspondents leaped to the defence of the traditional 'pig in the middle' position, although some wanted to have clear goals and roles. The popular alternative of 'issue-based work' needed to be 'earthed in projects' as earlier extensions of IM work had been earthed in works chaplaincy. The most stringent criticism of IM practice came from a Japanese academic, Shigeko Matsumoto, who had visited the UK in 1983 to study British IM. She identified three weaknesses and dangers of IM: 'clericalism, conformism and reductionism, all three of which are associated with the Chaplaincy model'. (28) She drew on an earlier unpublished thesis by Ted Lurkings which argued that a Church which opted for 'an inclusive role, blessing and embracing all aspects of society and ministered through priests could never perform the prophetic role'. The BSR published a brief summary of the thesis, with the conclusions in full. It was widely read by IM staff but seems not to have affected church policies nor teams' practices.

The debate continued in the pages of the *IMA Newsletter* in 1986. The Editor, Ian Stubbs, called for IM to move beyond 'issues' to 'engage in struggles with people'. This drew upon community organising programmes in the USA and Asia based on ideas of Saul Alinsky in *Rules for Radicals.* (29) Sister Mary McAleese, an Urban Mission worker in Liverpool and a member of the World Council of Churches – Urban Rural Mission (WCC-URM) committee contrasted her view of IM 'reconciling rich and poor, powerful and powerless' with the URM platform of 'calling the powerful to repentance'. (30) IMA Secretary Alison Norris thought that such a stance 'would get us thrown out'. (31)

IMA adopts 'The Way Forward' - but finds it hard to change

These issues were focussed at the 1988 IMA national conference. Three items came together in defining IM's stance at the time. A Filipino worker spoke of his experience and analysis of poverty. Christa Springe, at that time the staff member of ECG and a very experienced IM worker in West Germany, told how German IM had put pressure on a German company to settle a strike in their South Korean subsidiary. The third element was a study of the World

Council of Churches booklet, *Urban Rural Mission Reflections.* (32)
The conference (which had no formal place in the IMA Constitution)
passed a resolution called *The Way Ahead* with no contrary votes.
It concluded:

Therefore we commit ourselves;
1 to working alongside those who are oppressed and pushed
to the margins of society in order to enable them to take control
of their lives

2 to ensure that in all our dealings with people who have power
it is the concerns of the powerless which determine our
agenda. (The full resolution is quoted at Note 33.)

This resolution stimulated a number of projects within IM but there
is little evidence that it resulted in a major change of direction or
image. Teams were more engaged with the opportunities provided
by the publication later that year of *IM an Appraisal.* The publicity
and subsequent debate gave IM an opportunity to reconnect with
the churches. In those debates the pastoral side of IM was often the
only aspect to be praised, and a marked shift towards the more
radical WCC stance would not have been opportune. For many
teams their commitment to those marginalised by society was
through projects with and for the unemployed, which entailed
fitting in with Government funding regulations. Some had moved
on to engaging with local economic regeneration, supporting the
formation of cooperatives and community enterprises. Mostyn
Davies called this 'Mission in the Local Economy' or *Fourth
Generation IM.* (34) But IM would not or could not leave behind its
commitment to workplace ministry, with its inevitable compromises.
There was one specific outcome of that conference debate to which
we shall return in Chapter 5.

Industrial Mission an Appraisal (35)
A working party chaired by Peter Selby, then Bishop of Kingston,
and including three former or current industrial chaplains was set up
by the BSR in February 1986 and its report was presented to
General Synod in July 1988. Its task was to review the work of IM in
the 25 years since *The Task of the Church in Relation to Industry*
and make recommendations. Its members visited twelve IM teams.
They noted that the 1960s consensus had been set aside by the

Thatcher government, and that there were new deep divisions in Britain. Not least, the assumptions about the latent faith of working people had been replaced by what one Diocesan Bishop called the 'Godlessness of our nation' (p 1). The Report found an 'encouraging and vital picture of a movement widely connected with local people, structures and organisations, wrestling in committed and serious ways with the meaning of the Gospel in those situations' (p 10). However it also commented on the lack of a coherent strategy amongst teams, one of which was called 'a chorus of prima donnas'! (p 100) It speaks of '[IM] as an extended seminar in applied theology, conducted in an unfamiliar setting (the workplace) and with no guaranteed audience. In the process of clarifying its own mission it has raised issues about the mission of the whole church in the world' (p 49). IM's marginal status in the church meant that these issues were seldom effectively raised with the churches, nor did they influence the church's main missionary force in the world, the laity.

The Report proposed a structure to provide IM in each area with strategic management, together with a formal link to the Regional Ecumenical Council and through them to denominational leadership (p 102).

In addition to the Report three other booklets were produced by the BSR: *Dear Mr Green...* responses to it in correspondence with the BSR Chair; *Ministry and Mission Examined*, which gave further details of IM work including more recent styles of work. The third, *Church and Economy – Effective Industrial Mission for the 1990s* was the subject of the General Synod (GS) debate with the full report as an appendix. (36) This dealt with strategy and organisation at diocesan and national level, and issues of employment and training of IM staff. It urged Dioceses to link IM with the life of the Diocese particularly lay and ministerial training programmes. IM teams should be Local Ecumenical Projects under the auspices of County Sponsoring Bodies. Anglican IM staff should be seconded to these ecumenical teams.

In the General Synod debate the Archbishop of York spoke of 'the crucial and less accessible question of what Christianity means' which he said is the important question that IM asks the churches (GS report p 443). The Bishop of Southwark said 'in the

Report we now have a mission theology which comprehends both the personal dimensions of faith and the transformation of the unjust structures of society'. (GS report p 433). Two amendments to replace 'affirms IM's role' with 'acknowledges IM's role and criticisms expressed in the GS debate' were both lost. Apart from the speakers to those amendments every other speaker praised IM and supported the proposals. The only reservations were to plead for extra IM work in the City of London and in the growing service sector.

In many ways the Report and the GS debate may be seen as the high point in IM's history. At that time, and increasingly through the 1990s, the IM assumptions and practices were increasingly at odds with the political and industrial mainstream. Ten years of the Thatcher government, with the decimation of IM's originating industries of steel and coal, made it impossible to identify the 'central determining realities' with local manufacturing employers. Trades Unions focussed their energies on protecting jobs, strengthening their positions with their employers and moved away from discussions about wider social issues. International church bodies, not least the World Council of Churches, became more committed to the struggles of the poorest, and their understanding of such struggles in Liberation Theologies.

IM went into the 1990s buoyed up by the support given to *IM an Appraisal* and in some places new posts were created, particularly in retail and airports. However the political and economic changes steered by the Thatcher government had a marked effect on the industrial situation. The steel industry, the nursery of IM, had begun its route into the private sector after the strike in 1981 and plants continued to close or sharply reduce staffing. The closure programme for the coal industry begun in earnest in 1991 and by the end of the decade only a handful of mines survived. The decline of the engineering industry including motor manufacture was not as dramatic but equally devastating. IM debated the effects of the Single European Act of 1992 including the Social Charter and feared that increased competition would add to the effects of privatisation. Deregulation in transport and many local authority services also led to redundancies and pressure on wages. The argument that IM should work in and with these large scale employers began to lose its weight.

Increasing pressure on IM

In Britain churches, with many noble exceptions, turned their attention away from these almost insoluble problems, to renewed efforts in evangelism. The 1990s was the Decade of Evangelism (or Evangelisation for Roman Catholics). Support for liberal leaders and the social gospel waned and IM came under increasing criticism from evangelical parishes. The Church of England also faced financial pressures as its income from investments fell, particularly those by the Church Commissioners. In the years of growth Church of England chaplains' stipends came almost entirely from historic resources which could be applied by Diocesan Bishops as they chose. By 1990 a large and rapidly growing proportion of clergy stipends came from Diocesan budgets and were thus open to scrutiny and even control by Diocesan synods. Their income came from taxing parishes. This turned a critical spotlight on non-parochial posts. Parishes that feared that they could no longer have their own vicar, and at the same time were being asked to contribute more and more to the stipends budget, could easily request cuts in the staffing of non-parochial ministries. The crunch came in 1993 when, without consultation with the team or the other denominations, the Bishop of London announced the withdrawal of all seven Anglican posts from Church at Work in London, the IM team north of the Thames. All denominations experienced a reduction in stipendiary ministers, slightly offset by the growing number of ministers in secular occupations.

In 1991 the IMA Moderator John Paxton reported that many teams were being threatened with cuts in posts or the change from full-time to dual role. Even where posts were maintained teams reported increasing difficulty in filling them, further weakening the argument for continued funding. Many teams sought financial support from companies, and York Industrial Chaplaincy which was founded in 1998 was entirely paid for by the four companies served. In 1999 the Methodist Church abolished the office of National Officer in Mission in Business Industry and Commerce. The successive Secretaries to the Church of England's Industrial and Economic Affairs Committee had given considerable support to IM development from the first appointment in 1960 until 2001 when Ruth Badger left and the post was downgraded.

Is IM Mission?

IM had always seen itself as essentially ecumenical in character, and used the ecumenical structures to create and support teams as ecumenical partnerships. The county ecumenical structures set up as a result of the Churches Together in Pilgrimage process, seen in the transformation of 'The Coketown Council of Churches' to 'Churches Together in Coketown' at regional and national levels rarely developed the powers to oversee and support the ecumenical work of IM. In 2001 the Diocese of Sheffield, the Godparent of IM, tried unsuccessfully to dismantle the ecumenical structure of Industrial Mission in South Yorkshire (IMSY) and put the Anglican Chaplains under the direct authority of the Diocese. The Churches Consortium on Industrial Mission which had been a strong link between the IMA and the appropriate national officers of the denominations was replaced with a less authoritative consultative body Industrial and Economic Mission (INDEM). The IMA became one of the 'Bodies in Association with the Council of Churches in Britain and Ireland.' (CCBI)

The 1986 Brisbane statement by the world wide Anglican Mission agencies had given IM some text to link mission and evangelism (37), as had the Limuru statement earlier. But the documents produced for the churches' Decade of Evangelism had few connections to mission as understood and practised by IM. Antony Dalling called it 'a disembodied message'. (38) It was a sign that the mainstream of the churches was becoming preoccupied with its internal problems and loss of members to the exclusion of wider concerns. Faith in the City had produced an energetic focus on the problems of the inner cities; not least the very high levels of unemployment, and the Church Urban Fund helped local churches create many exciting projects. But when the CCBI report Unemployment and the Future of Work was published in 1997, calling on the political parties to put forward programmes to improve the lives of those in greatest need, it had little effect on either the churches or the politicians. (39)

Throughout the 1990s traditional long established workplace chaplaincies continued. The national coal industry network was able to lead the churches' campaign against the Heseltine closure programme, including a meeting with a junior minister led by the Bishop of Sheffield. As manufacturing industry declined many teams diversified into other sectors including retail, fire and rescue and the police services. Following the example of the Metro Centre in Gateshead, the first British Mall, chaplaincies were created in other major retail centres. The chaplain to the Bluewater Shopping Centre in Kent was appointed before the building was completed. The IMA In-Service Training Course grew in numbers and focussed on workplace chaplaincy. Many teams began to appoint part-time voluntary chaplains in these sectors. In these ways IM was adapting to the changed employment scene, and the sharp reduction in the number of full-time posts, and creating the model which would survive into the next decade.

Alongside this renewed emphasis on workplace models there were examples of work in the local economy. Leeds IM withdrew from its chaplaincy to the Leeds Cooperative store in order to focus on home-working; Sheffield created a post to stimulate community enterprises and in Lincoln Noel Beattie was instrumental in launching and supporting the Lincoln Enterprise Agency. As the Government created new regional bodies to stimulate regeneration by bringing together business leaders and local and national government officials, many chaplains found a new role growing out of their informal involvement with individual leaders. Some were offered seats on Training and Enterprise Councils and City Regeneration Agencies. In Luton industrial chaplain Martin Jones was invited to chair the Luton Economic Development Council, as someone who was acceptable to all the partners, the local authority, employers and trades unions. In Liverpool work continued to help unemployed people organise into campaigning groups and to represent redundant workers at Industrial Tribunals.

Many in the movement began to question the value of the title 'Industrial' in an increasingly post industrial society, in which teams operated in workplaces that did not see themselves as 'industrial'. Coventry IM renamed itself 'Mission in the World of Work'; Liverpool, seeing its field of operations in the wider sphere, became 'Mission in the Economy'; South Hampshire Industrial Mission became 'IBEX Churches working with the economy - Central South Coast'.

Two important studies of IM were published in 1992. A Swedish IM worker, Lillemor Erlander, wrote her PhD thesis *Faith in the world of work – worker priests (in France) and Industrial Mission (in Britain).* (40) She contrasts the 'secular spirituality' of both missionary projects with the 'spirituality of the official churches' in both countries. A review found it to be the best study of IM since Wickham. (41) By contrast, Michael Northcott's book *Church and Secularisation* (42) was critical of IM's 'disjunction between intentions and effects', a failing which had industry 'baffled'.

In 1994 Sheffield Industrial Mission celebrated its golden jubilee with an academic conference. Its purpose was to review the history and progress of Industrial Mission, and to ask searching questions about the nature of mission, spirituality and the Christian gospel in society. In addition to three plenary addresses by Bishop Peter Selby, Dr Anne Primavesi and Professor David McClellan workshop groups debated twelve papers mostly by industrial chaplains. These were edited by John Rogerson, Professor of Biblical studies at the University of Sheffield. He comments 'the church's function is to keep alive a vision that will sustain those who long and act to see God's goodness and justice established in the world. This biblical view of the church in relation to society has much to offer industrial mission'. (43)

At the end of the Millennium

In the last years of the Millennium the general pressure on the church's resources of staff and finance brought actual and threatened cuts in staffing. Teams had to work harder to justify their existence by playing a more active role in Diocesan and District Synods. Teams took accountability and management more seriously, and improved their publications. One further sign that IM was sharpening its practice could be seen when in 1999 Industrial Mission in South Yorkshire became the first church organisation in Britain to be awarded Investors in People status. This increased local focus had some effect on the time and finance to resource national activities. For example the Theological Development Group continued but was not able to turn its annual discussions into print. There were questions about its viability and it did not last long after the then Convenor Keith Wilson suddenly died in 1999.

In December 1995 the monthly in house *IMA Newsletter* was replaced with a more professional looking journal *IMAgenda*. Chris Warner, the first editor and full time chaplain in Great Yarmouth estimated that each issue took at least three days of his time, another example of IM's national model of collaboration. *IMAgenda* was planned to be of interest to people outside Industrial Mission.

Each month its 16 lithographed pages carried a Main Agenda Item (MAI), with news, analysis, theological reflection and usually (but not always) a report of work in hand by Chaplains. These MAIs ranged from Transport Deregulation, Europe, the Oil industry to Work/Life balance. Each issue also had worship materials as well as news from teams, though the latter occupied less space than in the *Newsletter*. Each year a special edition focussed on one theme which the IMA wanted to bring to the attention of church leaders, Mission, Worship and Spirituality were the first three. In January 1999 an IMA website was created alongside *IMAgenda,* which carried the journal's content together with further materials and links to many relevant web sites.

The Induction Course continued to recruit almost all new full time and an increasing number of part time staff. A pattern was developed of basing each of its three modules in different locations nationally, to draw on a wider variety of local inputs. Training materials were developed for teams and regions to use with those part time Chaplains who would be unable to attend the Induction course's three week long modules. In 1999 to undergird all this training a group produced *"Core skills for Workplace Chaplains".* Following a model commonly used in secular employment this set out 18 proficiencies under five headings – Theological, Economic, Practical, Pastoral and Prophetic (see Appendix to Chap 4).

As the Millennium ended it was clear that there was a future for a ministry to people in their workplaces, provided by lay and ordained chaplains coordinated and trained by a small number of full time or dual role leaders. The number and location would not only depend upon the supply of such volunteers but in some places upon the willingness of employers to contribute to the overall cost of the work. These teams would not have the time or other resources to manage the issue focussed projects that became possible in the 70s and 80s. They would have a small role in the training of ordained ministers, and in keeping on the church's agenda the ethical and political issues arising in the workplace. They would continue to be ecumenical though the ability of county ecumenical bodies to provide proper oversight would be limited. From the perspective of the man or woman meeting a Chaplain in their workplace it may not have seemed very different to their predecessors fifty years before. But IM was finding it much harder to make those grand claims about

IM "*working for the reordering of the relationships, methods and goals of industry and commerce, in the light of the Christian hope for justice and community*" (to quote the CCIM definition (18)).

Notes and references to this chapter

1 We have been unable to trace the source of this comment. Bishop A Winnington Ingram who became Bishop of London in 1901 rephrased it 'The Church of England has not lost the cities, she never had them.'

2 Malcolm Torry, *Bridgebuilders: Workplace Chaplaincy - a History,* Canterbury Press (2010) pp 36 and 43.

3 Donald M Ross, *God it's Monday,* St Andrew's Press (1997) p 8.

4 The Report of the Archbishop's Fifth Commission, *Christianity and Industrial Problems,1918*; quoted by S G Evans in *The Social Hope of the Christian Church,* Hodder and Stoughton (1965).

5 *Strategist for the Spirit,* edited by G Hewitt, Beckett (1985).

6 Paul Bagshaw, *Church beyond the Church,* IMSY (1994) traces the history of the work in Sheffield from 1944 to 1994. p 7.

7 Bagshaw, p 17.

8 D Gowland and S Roebuck, *Never call retreat – a biography of Bill Gowland,* Chester House Publications (1990) p 135.

9 E R Wickham, *Church and People in an Industrial City,* Lutterworth (1957).

10 *The Task of the Church in Relation to Industry,* CIO (1959).

11 *Growth and Inflation* (1975); *Powersharing in Industry* (1975);*Ethical Choice and Business Responsibilities* (1975); *Understanding Closed Shops* (1977); *Work and the Future* (1979); all CIO.

12 R Taylor, *Christians in an Industrial Society,* SCMP (1961) p 35.

13 *The Times,* 21 June 1966; *The Guardian,* 23 July 1966 quoted in Bagshaw pp 59 – 71.

14 J Robinson, *Honest to God,* SCMP (1963) p 25.

15 Bagshaw, p 67.

16 British Council of Churches, *The Church and Industry – an assessment of the need and the Response so far made Suggestions for advance,* BCC (1958).

17 Wickham, Appendix 4.

18 *Guidelines on the Task, Organisation, Appointments and Continuity of Industrial Mission,* Churches Consortium on Industrial Mission (1977).

19 Report of the Sixth Assembly of the World Council of Churches Vancouver, WCC (1984).

20 *IMA Newsletter,* March 1983, p 45.

21 The Report of the Archbishop's Commission on Urban Life and Faith, *Faith in the City,* CIO (1985).

22 Report of the Industrial Committee of the Board for Social Responsibility of General Synod, *Work and the Future,* CIO GS 429 (1979).

23 IMA Theology Development Group, *The End of Work?* William Temple Foundation (1980).

24 BSR, *The Church and the Miners' Strike,* CIO (1986).

25 *IMA Newsletter,* March 1983, p 31 and June 1983, p 68.

26 *Starting the Work,* CCIM (1982).

27 Review by I Stubbs, *IMA Newsletter,* December 1982; also January 1983, November 1984.

28 GS BSR, *A brief Summary of Shigeko Matsumoto's Thesis: A Critique of British Industrial Mission as a response of the Church in Modern Industrial Society,* BSR Industrial Affairs Committee IC/11/85 (1985).

29 Saul Alinsky, *Rules for Radicals,* Random House (1971).

30 *IMA Newsletter,* September 1986. For a brief outline of the WCC-URM desk policy which makes clear how far IM was from their position see *Urban Rural Mission Reflections,* WCC Commission on World Mission and Evangelism, Geneva (1986); and *A Community of Clowns – testimonies of people in Urban Rural Mission,* WCC Geneva (1987).

31 *IMA Newsletter,* September 1986.

32 *Urban Rural Mission Reflections,* WCC-CMWE. Amongst its statements was 'The Mission of God is action for transformation in the perspective of the kingdom', which should lead the church to participate in movements for 'organising for justice/organising for power' including 'the imperative of resistance'.

33 Report of the National Conference of the IMA held at Swanwick March 1988 Resolution, *The Way Forward:*

This conference acknowledges with gratitude the various contributions which have helped us in the process of renewing our vision, challenging the Church and seeing the way forward for Industrial Mission.

We believe that our Mission takes its pattern from Our Lord who unconditionally took sides with the suffering, weak and poor.

Therefore we commit ourselves;
1 to working alongside those who are oppressed and pushed to the margins of society in order to enable them to take control of their lives.
2 to ensure that in all our dealings with people who have power it is the concerns of the powerless which determine our agenda.

We urge IMA Regions and IM teams to endorse this statement and to propose the adoption of this stance to appropriate management bodies as a policy for the future.

We invite IMA Regions and Teams to study the WCC document URM Reflections to discover its implications for IM in their particular areas and then implement the recommendations.

34 Mostyn Davies *Industrial Mission – the anatomy of Crisis*, William Temple Foundation for the IMA TDG (1991).
35 *Industrial Mission – an Appraisal; the Church's Response to the Changing Industrial and Economic Order*, GS BSR CBF (1988).
36 *Dear Mr Green...; Ministry and Mission Examined; Church and Economy – Effective Industrial Mission for the 1990s* GS 886; all BSR (1989).
37 Quoted in *IMA Newsletter,* August 1991. It is worth including the full Limuru definition:

The obligation to make know to all men (sic) the name of their Saviour, to invite them into a personal commitment to him, and to build them up as active members of his liberating fellowship remains an enduring obligation. But this must necessarily be seen in the context of full involvement in God's contemporary work of liberation going beyond the boundaries of the Church otherwise the work of evangelism becomes a distortion of the Gospel. For the mission is God's mission: it concerns the whole of humanity and indeed the whole of creation. Quoted in GS153, *Today's Missionaries,* CIO 1973.

38 *IMA Newsletter,* April 1992.
39 Churches Together in Britain and Ireland, *Unemployment and the Future of Work – an Enquiry for the Churches,* CCBI (1997).
40 Lillemor Erelander, *Faith in the world of work – on the theology of work as lived by the French Worker-Priests and British Industrial Mission,* Uppsala University (1991) (in English).
41 *IMA Newsletter,* January 1992.
42 Michael Northcott, *The Church and Secularisation: Urban Industrial Mission in North-East England,* Peter Lang, Bern (1989); reviewed in *IMA Newsletter,* July 1992.
43 Edited by J Rogerson, *Industrial Mission in a Changing World – Papers from the Jubilee Conference of the Sheffield Industrial Mission,* Sheffield Academic Press (1996).

CHAPTER TWO

The Original Theology of Industrial Mission

*'The Kingdom of heaven is to me the great
existing reality which is to renew the earth*
Frederick Denison Maurice

For Industrial Mission, as arguably for all projects in Christian mission at their best, theology has provided the crucial intellectual and spiritual impetus. This chapter first sketches thinking and practice about mission in Britain in the early and mid-twentieth century, in order to appreciate the theological context in which Leslie Hunter was nurtured before he became Bishop of Sheffield in 1939. Hunter's own theological and evangelistic vision is considered in some detail, as is contemporary thinking and practice about Christian ministry in factories. It was Hunter's inspiration, of course, to invite Ted Wickham to begin work as Industrial Chaplain in that city, and the aims and pattern of Wickham's work are described for the theology which was integral to them, not least his conviction that Christian mission and ministry to the estranged working people of Britain would only become deep-rooted and sustainable if it were led by some of the same lay people. Finally some of the great theological themes which animated this work and the Christian thinkers who provided them are described.

The missiological context in Britain in which Industrial Mission grew

The British Churches struggled to respond to the massive effects of urbanisation and industrialisation in the nineteenth and early twentieth centuries. Working people who had moved to the cities had never attended church very much. Clergy who became army chaplains during the First World War discovered the great gulf between working-class men and the churches, which were perceived as only for educated and middle-class people. A chaplain who really learnt how to communicate with ordinary people – and particularly when they were facing the terrifying, life-changing experience of the Western Front – was Geoffrey Studdert-Kennedy, who soon became known and loved as 'Woodbine Willie' from his habit of sharing his cigarettes with the troops. His dialect poems about the brutal realities of war became famous – he had realised the basic truth that in order to communicate with people you have got to speak their language.

After that War in 1919 the Industrial Christian Fellowship (ICF) was founded, a coming together of the activist Navvy Mission Society and the more intellectual Christian Social Union, and Studdert-Kennedy was invited to become General Secretary. He became a sought-after evangelist, and under his leadership ICF employed a number of lay Missioners who gave addresses at organised 'street corner' meetings and in factories. ICF also ran educational correspondence courses and published a monthly journal which reached a circulation of 30,000. However, Philip Bloy comments that Studdert-Kennedy appeared to have 'reservations about any social reformism which looked as if it might neglect a man's individual need for redemption', and – in the light of later theological insights – the missioners seemed rather over-confident in the relevance of Christian faith for industrial people, instead of hoping to discover that relevance in the process of working in that context. (1)

Prominent in Christian concern for the shape and direction of society in Britain in the inter-war years were Richard Tawney, William Temple, and J H Oldham. Tawney was Professor of Economic History at London University, and his writings were very influential. He was both a committed Anglican and a socialist, and believed that in the wake of the widespread economic failures of those years a fundamental change in the values and structure of society was required. A just society would have a tendency towards greater equality.

William Temple (1881 – 1944) was of course an outstanding Archbishop of Canterbury, but his commitment to social reform can be seen early in the fact that he was the first President of the Workers Educational Association (1908 -24). He also was the chairman of the Conference on Christian Politics, Economics and Citizenship (1924), which attracted 1,500 delegates and had great effect on the Ecumenical Movement. (2) Both within and outside the churches he became perhaps most widely known for his *Christianity and Social Order,* published in 1942. (3) In it Temple sets economic policy within a moral framework for society as a whole, and ended with a statement of six objectives which Christians should call on government to pursue – concerning family life, education, income, employee involvement in the management of industry, leisure and liberty.

J H Oldham (1874 – 1969) was secretary to the international ecumenical conference held in Edinburgh in 1910, and became an important ecumenical figure. He was a leader in the 'Life and Work' movement, which between the two World Wars encouraged practical joint activities amongst the churches, and in 1948 joined with the Faith and Order Movement to become the World Council of Churches. Oldham was also largely responsible for setting up the Christian Frontier Council. 'Frontier' was defined as the place where the Christian meets the world, and where Christian Faith meets other systems of thought. Oldham edited the Council's *Christian Newsletter* 1939 – 1948: this aimed to equip its readers to think theologically about the contemporary secular world.

Bishop Leslie Hunter comes to Sheffield

One of the enthusiastic members of the Christian Frontier Council was Leslie Hunter, who had been appointed Bishop of Sheffield in 1939. Hunter's father had been a Congregationalist minister with a particular appreciation of the theology of Frederick Denison Maurice (1805 – 1872), one of the influential Anglican thinkers of the nineteenth century. This appreciation was clearly passed on to Hunter, who made frequent references to it in his addresses. Part of the appeal of Maurice's thought lies in the fact that his theology does **not** begin in the sinfulness of humankind (as did so many other Christian leaders of his age), but in God's tremendous love, specifically that God has created and redeemed human beings in Christ. Justice, truth and love all have their sources in God's will. 'The Kingdom of heaven', he said, 'is to me the great existing reality which is to renew the earth'. (4) Maurice was not only a theologian but a political activist: he was a leader of the Christian Socialist group from 1848 – 54, and stated that God's Law must be acknowledged in economic conditions as well as all other areas of human life.

Hunter had come to Sheffield from a great deal of experience of Christian ministry in the urban areas of Newcastle and Barking. In

1941 Hunter's Letter to his Diocese was particularly important, in that it contains his analysis of local church life and his vision for future Christian policies. The Letter began with the results of a survey done in an industrial area of Sheffield with a population of 50-60,000. Hunter was appalled by the statistics of church attendance, and must have been aware that other areas were not much better. Even making allowance for the 'diffused Christianity amongst non-churchgoers' he draws the conclusion that England had 'become once again a mission field – the conditions not unlike those which confronted the Wesleys', though with a difference; this time any mission would be to people for whom the Gospel is no longer fresh. (5) The Church needs to respond with evangelism, but it must be a better quality of evangelism. 'Every member of the Church must have it burnt into his mind that the Church is set in the world to redeem it – never for a moment to be a pious clique keeping itself to itself – but a saving, serving apostolic society.' Evangelism will be fruitful if it is based on 'a firmly-held and well-understood doctrine of God and man' with a 'warm, convinced devotion' to Christ. The Gospel must not be sentimentalised and needs to be expressed in fresh language, because the usual language had become tired and conventional. This new evangelism would have to be far more than 'a speaking war'; it would have to be a comprehensive witness of daily living, prayer and social action. How well equipped were local churches for this task, and how clear and relevant was the message of the clergy? 'Finally, the new evangelism will be more than a recall. It will look forward to a new order both in church and in society'. (6) Hunter was clearly calling for a Christian initiative which would include individual responses to Christ, the renewing of congregations, and the transformation of whole communities.

Hunter and many others were aware that one of the great hindrances to the Gospel was that much working-class culture had grown up outside the churches. Further there were working-class suspicions that the churches were simply being used as a tool of the capitalist and managerial class. The idea that a few clergy could have direct contact with people at work in factories to tackle this cultural gulf was being discussed in the early 1940s. Ian Fraser, a newly-ordained minister in the Church of Scotland, spent six months in 1942-3 as an employee in a Fife paper mill, and later wrote about his experience in the *Christian Newsletter*. He found the great cultural divide between the Church and working people to be present everywhere, but 'working with men in the mill here, these masks have been ripped aside ...What counts most with men is the way in which you measure up to life as you rub shoulders with them. It is in silent ways, the ways of character and of prayer, that the most effective witness is made'. (7) Fraser realised that the Church clearly needed to affirm all that was valuable in the lives of working people before attempting to talk about the Gospel. In a reflection published in 1944 he advocated that Christian ministers should not only *visit* people in workplaces, but *work alongside them* on the shop-floor or in the offices. (8)

Beginning organised Christian ministry in factories, and its pastoral and theological rationale

Wartime conditions hastened the appointment of the first full-time workplace chaplains, especially in the large Royal Ordnance Factories which were built to produce much-needed munitions, often in rural areas. So at the end of 1941 a young priest called Ted Wickham, fresh from his curacy in Shieldfield, Newcastle, was appointed as chaplain to the largest of them, at Swynnerton (Staffordshire). Wickham had studied for an external Bachelor of Divinity degree at London University before going to theological college, and particularly enjoyed reading the nineteenth century existential Danish theologian Soren Kierkegaard, as his works were translated into English. Kierkegaard is well known for describing the decision to become a Christian as 'the leap of faith', and how that must have resonated for Wickham as he began this ministry of outreach.

At the Swynnerton factory as many as 20,000 people worked filling shells and detonators in clearly hazardous work, and working three shifts round the clock. Since the chaplain's presence on the shop floor was impossible, owing to the tight security and hazards, most of the ministry was in the hostels which were largely populated by women. Wickham was convinced of the need to provide forums for discussion and instruction, and was working out a strategy which he later operated among study groups in Sheffield. Gradually he and a few colleagues built up in each of the five large hostels on the site little groups of Christians who worshipped together and worked out strategies and techniques for giving Christianity a higher profile there. Ted later married one of his chaplaincy colleagues – Helen Moss, who had come to the factory as a labour officer.

Meanwhile in Sheffield Hunter had not been idle. His Diocesan Letter of February 1944 mentions a Committee of Anglican and Free Church ministers in Sheffield to deal with 'Works' Padres'. A short training conference was arranged in which the basis of this work was briefly stated: God created human beings to work, and so the Lordship of Christ and the power of God had to be realised in work as in all other areas of life; clergy needed to learn about and share in the life of workers, and to share Christ with them.

In early 1944 the British Council of Churches organised a conference on industrial chaplaincies, in which doubts were expressed about whether it would be right to continue chaplaincies to wartime factories after the war had ended. Would there be any need if the munitions factories were going to close? Surely it would be better for parochial clergy to increase their contacts with the factories in their areas. Joe Oldham reviewed the conference in the *Christian Newsletter*, and questioned whether local clergy were all well suited for this work. He believed that the conference had not taken seriously enough the reality of the cultural gulf between church life and industrial life. In a supplement to this *Newsletter* Oldham printed the views of Michael Dean, Industrial Secretary of the Student Christian Movement: he said that the real work was not holding services but making contacts in the production departments, and as a result the barriers between the Church and working people were slowly being removed. 'The authority of the Church counts for nothing in the works; a man must stand on his own merits'. (9) In the midst of this debate, Bishop Hunter announced in April 1944 the appointment of Ted Wickham 'to be an Industrial Chaplain in the Diocese, and to help make contacts within the industries as he is invited.' As a good bishop he gave Wickham the names of some of the senior managers he knew, including that of the Managing Director of Firth Vickers Stainless Steels Ltd., Eric Holstrom. Ted got permission to visit freely in the works, made contact with the appropriate trade union officials, and was away.

Holmstrom

Just because the idea of clergy visiting some factories and workplaces had been discussed in some church circles did not mean it was at all familiar to the great majority of people outside the churches, of course. A great many people at Firth Vickers were surprised to see Wickham, perhaps puzzled, and not a little intrigued. *What was he there to do?* It was a question which went to

34

the heart of the task of Christian theology and mission in which Wickham was engaged.

He always wore his clerical collar, so people knew **what** he was. He was there to meet them, first of all, to take them and their jobs seriously – but he did not come without being prepared to have something to say. If individual workers were prepared to give him some of their time, they were entitled to expect 'their money's worth', he would say. Although Wickham spent a great deal of his time with manual workers (because it seemed clear that their alienation from the churches and formal faith was greatest), he also paid regular visits to the offices, and to the managers of the departments he visited. He quickly developed the device of the 'meeting', an informal discussion session in the corner of the workshop - which might begin with a comment or question from someone present – or if not, Wickham himself would always be prepared to introduce a topic. These meetings, arranged in advance by someone in that workshop friendly to the idea, became a regular feature of his work. They were both occasions when the reality of industrial life came face to face with the reality of Wickham's Christian faith, but also when those who were attracted by his approach to faith and life also became apparent. From early on he began to form a group of people who wanted to talk for much longer than the 20 minutes or so available for workshop meetings. So on Thursday evenings, a group would meet in his home and continued to meet òn that evening for the whole time Wickham was in Sheffield. ⟍ Later at Church House

Wickham's aim in developing this network of groups, which grew greatly as the Mission itself expanded, was (in the words of Philip Bloy) to make this whole Christian work **indigenous**, 'in such a way that persons in industry themselves might share by taking on leadership roles, so that the mission might be **their** mission and not just the padre's'. (10) In 1950 all members of the Thursday and Sunday groups were challenged to 'make a step forward and grow into the Church'. This would entail 'coming over the line as committed Christians' – which would include worshipping together, studying together, planning the mission together, and enjoying fellowship with each other. (11) In 1955 a 'Second Line' conference was held at William Temple College, Rugby. The 'front line' consisted of lay people who were undertaking mission in the works in their daily work; the 'second line' were those who would train, encourage and support them. (12) Christian lay leaders in the works were a crucial stage towards 'the Church outside the Church'. It is frustrating that records of the work of these lay-led groups have not survived, but we can be certain that they spent their time both discussing current issues in the works, industry or local community, and also seeking relevant help from Bible passages.

Thus this whole lay development was an integral part of industrial mission, stemming from Wickham's conviction that the only way to overcome the generations of working-class indifference or hostility to the church and Christian faith would be to plant an **indigenous** Christian mission within this great sector of society which could communicate the Gospel in terms which everyone there could understand. It is surely the only way to produce sustainable Christian mission and ministry in any sector of society with a distinctive culture. As Philip Bloy memorably puts it: 'the task was not to make industry Christian but to make Christianity industrial. Put that way, the Church becomes truly incarnated and only then effectively contributes and ministers'. (13)

The question now arises: should this work, undertaken first by Wickham and then also increasingly by others, be correctly termed *evangelism*? There was a clear introduction of Christian themes and values in factory discussions, however much this was deliberately done in the context of contemporary issues, both local and national. Invitations to develop further a Christian understanding of life and society were often issued, in the shape of the opportunity to join the weekly evening study groups, and once a month this meeting was preceded by a celebration of Holy Communion in Sheffield Cathedral. There is evidence that a clear group for Christian worship and study had emerged: Bagshaw reports that from 1955 to July 1958 the numbers attending these services varied from 20-30, whereas July 1958 to July 1960 attendance had risen from 30-50. (14) Such groups would, in the present British context and in the wake of the well-known Anglican report *Mission-shaped Church* (15) undoubtedly be termed a 'fresh expression' of church.

On the face of it, therefore, it seems strange that Wickham should have permanently repudiated the word *evangelism* – and Philip Bloy takes him to task for so doing. Bloy acknowledges that the word had taken on a very individualist meaning, and some would regard it as being very loaded towards an emotional rather than an intellectual appeal. Bloy comments: 'To eschew that word so as to distance ministry in industry from such an inadequate approach was understandable in the opening phases of a mission, but to shun it in perpetuity was to allow industrial mission to develop with an impoverished outlook'. (16) Part of that impoverishment was to raise tensions with other clergy and Christians who regarded evangelism as a key task of the Church, and thus to give a theological hostage to fortune which would, in the context of a later distinctly evangelical leadership both of the Sheffield Industrial Mission and the Diocese, lead to the break-up of the existing Sheffield team in 1965.

Anyone who has been in the position of having to negotiate Christian chaplaincy to a secular community in modern Britain – industrial or otherwise – knows that to state clearly that the aim of the project is to do evangelism would be to risk instant rejection. Evangelism in the minds of many people is the 'hard selling' of Christianity, putting people under pressure to believe in salvation through Jesus Christ. This was as true in Wickham's time as it is 65 years later. On the other hand, for an industrial chaplain to deny that he or she aimed to present Christian faith in an attractive way through making relationships in the workplace, in the hope that (as one of the aims) some people might eventually make quite voluntarily a commitment of faith in Jesus Christ – this would surely lead to some people questioning the reason for the church to employ such a person!

Evangelism therefore remained – and arguably remains – a difficult concept for Industrial Mission to handle, but perhaps the way forward is to explicitly reject associations with large evangelistic rallies and emotional appeals for conversion, and to return to a more Biblically-based definition: the process of conveying the good news of God's Kingdom, the liberation of humankind from the terrible constraints of sin, suffering and death. As Bloy comments: 'Industrial Mission is evangelisation in the full meaning of that word. If not, it isn't industrial mission'. (17)

The Theological impetus – perceiving God's action in the challenges and confusion

Thus Christian mission and ministry to this huge section of British society which had been moulded by the nineteenth century industrial revolution, by massive urbanisation, frequent industrial conflict and endemic poverty, began in earnest. The task was enormous, because the churches were often not seen as relevant to the real world in which everyone had to live. Many clergy and lay Christians must have found great events such as the massive economic recession which led to acute unemployment in the 1930s, and the terrible privations and ambiguities of the Second World War, very confusing and challenging. So what drove the first industrial missioners?

The first great theological theme was that the living God was not to be found by using the church and the Christian faith as a refuge from the confusion and challenge of the world around them, but rather by trying to understand all the changes taking place, and seeing in them God at work. Of course Christians still needed to take seriously the truths of the faith, and to learn from the Bible about the ways in which God is active, but these enable Christians to recognise and discern God's hand in contemporary events and situations. The American pastor and theologian Paul Tillich (1886 – 1965) published a volume of sermons in 1949 called *The Shaking of the Foundations,* which was important for those involved in early industrial mission. Tillich was a German academic who, as an outspoken critic of the Nazi regime, was forced to leave Germany in 1933, and went to live in the United States and teach theology there. He developed an 'apologetic' type of sermon largely for non-church people. He asserted boldly that, far from being a refuge from all the challenge and confusion in the world, it is **God who causes** all the disturbance in the world, and he based this on an exegesis of passages in Jeremiah and Isaiah. It is only as the whole world of human achievement is disturbed that the eternal is made visible. (18) Given the events he had lived through, it is not surprising that Tillich found great hope and resource in the prophets whose faith had been shaped through times of great destruction and change.

Given the belief that God is working through all sorts of events in the world, both on an international and on a local level, constructing a reliable and workable method of discerning God's activity amidst the chaos and complexity of world events became important. Tillich's 'method of correlation' became useful here, and at least one chaplain recruited by Wickham testifies to its use in the original Sheffield team. (19) In a passage from his *Systematic Theology I,*

Tillich explains that the method involves making an analysis of the human situation, and demonstrating that the elements of the Christian faith are the answers to these questions. 'If anxiety is defined as the awareness of being finite, God must be called the infinite ground of courage ... If the notion of the Kingdom of God appears in correlation with the riddle of our historical existence, it must be called the meaning, fulfilment and unity of history.' (20) In Chapter 3 further attempts in industrial mission to construct workable methods of discerning God's activity in the world and to understand its meaning are described.

Tillich's *Systematic Theology,* which appeared in three volumes from 1953 to 1964, also helped some of the early industrial missioners to clarify the Church's task and role in a secular world. In an interesting passage in his *Church and People in an Industrial City,* Wickham refers to Tillich's typology of the relationship between the Church and the surrounding world. 'Theonomy' describes the situation in which the Church accurately reflects the whole life of the Christian community, and the secular community completely embodies Christian values. This idealised picture has often degenerated into mere religious conformity. 'Heteronomy' is the situation in which a 'theocratic' church refuses any adaptation to society, which it regards as secular and even hostile. The third mode of relationship, which can be described as 'autonomy', describes a situation in which the Church is aware of belonging to the surrounding world, yet has a vital role as a catalyst within the world, 'to understand it, prophesy within it, interpret it and stain it.' Wickham clearly regarded 'autonomy' as the inevitable and proper relationship of a Church to a world 'determined to be master of its own destiny'. (21) Tillich visited Wickham in Sheffield in March 1957, and later the same year the two met again when Wickham went to the United States on a lecture tour.

It is one thing to speak of the desirability of seeing God at work in the great events of the twentieth century – just as Second Isaiah spoke of God moving through the power of the emperor Cyrus to punish Babylon and release God's people from their exile. It is quite another thing to help Christians in the task of discerning what God is doing in particular events, and what is the right course of action to take in a difficult situation. Chapter 3 sets out some ways in which those engaged in later industrial mission developed some answers to these questions. But the early pioneers in Sheffield and elsewhere looked eagerly for guidance to some of the great contemporary ethicists and theologians. Reinhold Niebuhr (1892 – 1971) originally published *Moral Man and Immoral Society* in 1932. (22) The very title recalls the important distinction which Niebuhr makes between the behaviour of individual human beings and that of human groups, communities or nations. He shows that individuals are quite able to consider the interests of others, and even of giving preference to them in many situations; whereas such capacity is very difficult if not impossible for human groups, which almost always express the perceived self-interests of the group. As he was writing, the world was suffering from economic depression, causing tremendous poverty which in turn was giving rise to fascist governments in Italy and (soon) in Germany. Niebuhr pleads for a political morality which will do justice both to ethical values and political realism, and will try to save society from being involved in endless cycles of futile conflict. As Ronald Preston points out (23), he shows the importance of the insights of the traditional Christian doctrine of humanity for individuals and groups, something Niebuhr later developed in *The Nature and Destiny of Man* (1941 – 43).

The theological impetus – understanding and living the Gospel as twentieth century people

The Sheffield team under Wickham's leadership not only were eager to use contemporary theological thinking in the service of their work, but were also not slow to share it with those they met in the course of their work. Bagshaw reports that factory workers wrote to Rudolf Bultmann about the whole issue of 'demythologising' Christian belief at a time when such questions were rarely raised outside academic journals. (24) It is useful to give a brief explanation of this topic so that its relevance for the early work of industrial mission can be appreciated. Rudolf Bultmann (1884 – 1976) taught Theology at the University of Marburg for 30 years until 1951. He is probably best remembered for his efforts to separate the Christian gospel from the mythological concepts and language in which it is expressed in the New Testament ('demythologising'). As Josh Reeves points out (25), Bultmann can be most positively seen as reacting against nineteenth-century German theological liberals such as Adolf Harnack, who believed that Jesus' significance lay only in his moral teachings. With Karl Barth, Bultmann argues that the New Testament witnesses to an event which has achieved our salvation, and not primarily to a moral teacher. At the same time, Bultmann could not in any way follow Barth's strict acceptance of the Biblical text, with the mythological world which Biblical authors took for granted. How can people living in a modern scientific culture accept a mythical world as true? That culture tells people that supernatural powers cannot interrupt the laws of cause and effect; any reference to supernatural actions (including miracles, for example) has made the mistake of objectifying that which is transcendent. Bultmann extensively used the existentialism of Martin Heidegger as the philosophy which most accurately understands human life; so for him the Christian gospel is that God has liberated humanity from 'our factual fallenness in the world' so that we can now live authentically as human beings. (26)

Pursuing this process of demythologising, living 'according to the Spirit' does not refer to any supernatural influence for Bultmann, but describes 'a genuine human life' which lives from 'what is invisible and non-disposable, and therefore surrenders all self-contrived security'. (27) The achievement of Jesus was not in the apparent placating of a wrathful God, but in the fact that through him 'our authentic life becomes a possibility in fact for us only when we are freed from ourselves'. (28) To factory workers meeting the first industrial missioners, workers whose whole lives were dominated and arguably diminished by the industrial situation, the possibility of authentic human life in spite of any set of crushing circumstances was indeed very meaningful.

Whilst Bultmann's radical interpretation of the New Testament may have upset many traditionalist Christians, Wickham and other missioners seized on such material as greatly facilitating the task of explaining the meaning of Jesus and the world of the Bible to so many outside the churches - who could scarcely understand the English of the King James Version, let alone the thought-world of 2,000 years ago (and needed to be convinced that this task was worth the effort!). *Kerygma and Myth* by Bultmann and Five Critics was published in English in 1953, and must have been a real gift to the work in Sheffield and elsewhere – although of course the more the process of demythologising Christian belief was used in industrial mission work, the greater the eventual controversy with traditionalist Christians in other parts of the Church.

The other towering theological mind which seemed to identify with the dilemma of twentieth century people needing to accept scientific explanations for the world, and yet also needing to reach out in hope and trust to that which is beyond science, belonged to Dietrich Bonhoeffer (1906 – 1945). He was a far-sighted Christian minister and theologian who was instrumental in setting up the Confessing Church in Germany in 1936, breaking away from the mainstream Lutheran Church because of its support for Hitler's government. The Confessing Church courageously opposed that regime, and Bonhoeffer himself was arrested and imprisoned in 1943. During the next two years he wrote the letters and reflections which became *Letters and Papers from Prison*. He was executed for his continuing opposition to Hitler's regime in April 1945, one month before Germany's surrender.

Bonhoeffer was dominated by the whole issue of Christian belief and practice in the modern world, and curiously enough he refers to Bultmann's essay on demythologising the New Testament.

It's not only the 'mythological' concepts, such as miracle, ascension, and so on ... but 'religious' concepts generally, which are problematic. You can't, as Bultmann supposes, separate God and miracle, but you must be able to interpret and proclaim both in a 'non-religious' sense. (29)

A few days earlier he had written in another letter to Eberhard Bethge (married to his niece Renate):

What is bothering me incessantly is the question what Christianity really is, or indeed who Christ really is, for us today ... We are moving towards a completely religionless time; people as they are now simply cannot be religious any more ...How can Christ become the Lord of the religionless as well? If religion is only a garment of Christianity ... then what is a religionless Christianity? (30)

To industrial missioners trying to communicate the essence of the Gospel to virtually religionless industrial workers, this key question was very helpful. It was almost as if God was demolishing the traditional religious world-view, and both missioners and the church as a whole had to change their perspective if they were ever to get the Christian message across. Bonhoeffer did not give many clues about charting the way forward in this new situation – tragically, he did not live long enough for that. However, defining the whole issue in this way many people found creative, including John Robinson, who wrote his famous book *Honest to God* (31) a few years later in a time of theological ferment. One biographer of Bonhoeffer sums up the great issue of his theology in this way:

The task before the Church today, clearly foreseen by Bonhoeffer, is that of becoming fully identified with the modern world without losing her Christian identity. Bonhoeffer is quoted continually as the prophet of identification; that he was equally concerned with the Christian's identity is commonly forgotten. (32)

So early industrial mission was determined to use the best contemporary theological resources which lay to hand in a threefold task. Firstly, to identify with the confusions and challenges of people in the 1940s and 50s – enormous changes in society, in science, in the economy, and in morality; secondly, trying to understand the spiritual needs of people in the context of these changes and challenges; thirdly, trying to communicate the message of what God has done and is still doing in Jesus Christ so that it can genuinely be good news to people living in this context in the mid-twentieth century. This was inevitably a risky undertaking, for in an important sense theologians like Tillich, Niebuhr, Bultmann and Bonhoeffer were at times feeling their way forward, using their best abilities to understand what God is doing in the world, how he works and how best this may be communicated, and yet knowing that there could be no complete certainty. At the same time, the early industrial missioners knew that they were attempting something very difficult – no less than the overcoming of several centuries of alienation from the Christian community and Gospel, and the planting of many new, lively and sustainable Christian groups. The risk of failure and of being misunderstood was immense. In the circumstances, the conflicts which were generated between the early Sheffield team and other parish clergy there, as well as amongst that team itself during the leadership of Michael Jackson and the episcopate of John Taylor, were only to be expected. The resulting break-up of that team in 1965, whilst very painful for those involved and the many affected in Sheffield, arguably had a very beneficial effect on the spread and the quality of industrial mission work in Britain in the next 25 years.

Notes and references to this chapter

1. Philip Bloy, *The Call to Mission Answered,* Disciples Press (2000) p 10.
2. F A Iremonger, *William Temple* (Abridged edition by D C Somervell, 1. 1963) p 155.
3. Later published by Penguin Books as a Pelican in 1956.
4. Quoted in Bloy, p 13.
5. Quoted in Michael Atkinson, *Theological Influences in the Early Years of Industrial Mission* p 8, essay in *Thinking in Practice,* Working Papers from Industrial Mission No. 3, IMA Theology Development Group (1981).
6. Quoted in Atkinson, p 9.
7. Ian Fraser's article 'Masks and Men' published as supplement to *The Christian Newsletter* No.187, July 1943.
8. Radio talk 'A Padre in a Scottish Factory', published in Ian Fraser *My Faith and my Job,* Epworth Press (1944).
9. Quoted in Atkinson, p 14.
10. Bloy, p 11.
11. The full document is included in Paul Bagshaw, *The Church beyond the Church,* Industrial Mission in South Yorkshire (1994) p 22-24.
12. Bagshaw, pp 29-30.
13. Bloy, p 85.
14. Bagshaw, pp 31-32.
15. *Mission-shaped Church,* a report of a working group of the Church of England's Mission and Public Affairs Council, chaired by Rt Revd Graham Cray (Bishop of Maidstone), Church House Publishing (2004).
16. Bloy, pp 85-86.
17. Bloy, p 86.
18. Paul Tillich, *The Shaking of the Foundations,* Penguin Books (1962) pp 11-20.
19. Michael Atkinson, who was recruited by Wickham, and chaplain in Sheffield Industrial Mission 1960-66, in personal reflections to be found at the website www.industrialmissionhistory. org.uk
20. Paul Tillich, *Systematic Theology I*, pp 69-72, quoted in E J Tinsley, *Paul Tillich,* Epworth Press (1973).
21. *Church and People in an Industrial City*, pp 229-230. Wickham does not himself describe the third mode of relationship as

'autonomy', but it seems an accurate description. In the same passage he calls Christians 'free men, men of their age, and members of an autonomous culture'. In *Systematic Theology* Tillich uses the theonomous/heteronomous/autonomous typology several times. See also Chapter 7 section headed 'The essential basis will be a Kingdom Theology'.

22. Published in the United States. The first British edition did not appear until 1963, published by SCM.
23. In a note in the first British edition.
24. Bagshaw, p 29.
25. Josh Reeves, *Rudolf Bultmann and Demythologization,* internet article, (2005).
26. Bultmann, *New Testament and Mythology and other Basic Writings,* Fortress Press (1984) - quoted by Reeves p 26.
27. Bultmann, – quoted by Reeves, p 17.
28. Bultmann, – quoted by Reeves, p 30.
29. Dietrich Bonhoeffer, *Letters and Papers from Prison,* ed. Eberhard Bethge, SCM Press London (1971) p 285.
30. Bonhoeffer, reference above, pp 279-280.
31. John A T Robinson, *Honest to God,* SCM Press (1963).
32. Mary Bosanquet, *The Life and Death of Dietrich Bonhoeffer,* Hodder & Stoughton (1968) p 279.

CHAPTER THREE

Theological and Ethical
Development Within Industrial Mission

*Theology talking to itself demonstrates
a high parody of a high calling to inform
and energise the people of God for faithful living*

Paul Ballard and John Pritchard, *Practical Theology in Action*,
SPCK (1996)

The core of IM practice was debate, often in an unusual setting for such topics but nonetheless serious and probing. Chaplains were asked 'what do you think?' about a wide range of subjects from the existence of God to the current wage claim. As they became more accepted in the workplace they would create their own agenda of questions, seeking to deepen or widen the scope of debate. To do so they drew on the theology and social ethics which they had studied in their training. Many were able debaters who could connect their theology to everyday issues in language sufficiently secular to communicate with industrial workers. The mid-twentieth century interest in secular interpretations of the gospel helped them do so. However the general ethical statements which the churches had created in the thirties were usually couched in terms of policy rather than practicalities. This chapter shows how IM sought to apply theology and ethics to the situations in which they were working. Because the need arose in the situation, rather than prior to their entry, they generally used inductive rather than deductive methods.

There were two underlying questions, 'How do we discern God's presence and activity in the world?' and, 'How should we respond?' The Mission's practice was based on the premise that God was already at work in the world. The first generation of IM staff based their work on a world affirming theology and laid the foundations for those who followed them. As we outlined in Chapter 2 they struggled to find appropriate secular words to convey their faith and this became a cornerstone of the IM tradition. Individuals and teams studied widely both to buttress their faith and to explain their activities to people in industry and in the churches.

Creating an inductive theology

In December 1970 the William Temple College Rugby acted as host for a three-day study conference based on those underlying questions. Two groups worked at the problem in different ways. One developed the theoretical models of the ways faith could interact with the secular world. They began by studying contemporary theologians who were reworking aspects of Natural Theology. Richard Niebuhr in *Christ and Culture* (1) identified one mode of the Christian hope for the world in the phrase 'Christ will, can and must convert culture'. Peter Berger in *A Rumor of Angels* (2) identified five signposts in secular experience which point to 'another dimension'. The group concluded that an inductive model was both possible and necessary. They observed that the optimism of the post-war world was being eroded by growing managerialism, focussed on economic success above all else. They were searching for a theology which would help them speak about the Kingdom of God to secular people and would provide hope for a different model of society. They also recognised that this theological model was but one amongst many available.

The second group studied three current issues in order to test the model. The issues were boring work (especially high volume assembly line situations), the Government's Industrial Relations Bill (which led to the Industrial Relations Act 1971) and company responsibility (at a time when companies were merging, growing in size and become international). Applying the model to 'boring work' they affirmed the need for workers to find ways to maintain their humanity in the face of their inhuman situation. They saw the need for a new legal framework for industrial relations which should be realistic 'seeing man as he is' (sic). But the law should not only take that position but also encourage managers and trades unions 'to live as if something better is possible'. The group on 'company responsibility' used biblical models of the body, and of Israel to stress the interdependence and thus shared responsibility of every part of a business organisation. We shall return to these issues later in this chapter.

Papers from the conference were taken to the IMA National Conference in 1971. (3) Archbishop Michael Ramsey, one of the keynote speakers, said that,

> *he had been conscious all along that IM is a theological adventure which was discovering things about theology from which the rest of the church could learn ... but that he felt that the inductive method would only be effective if those who practice it had deep within themselves the timeless truths declared by the church's teaching.*

He warned IM against over reliance on inductive theology alone. 'It is a process of reflection through which you may only get a reflection of yourself!' Margaret Kane also commented 'when Christians move out towards those who are estranged from God and from the Church, trying to see life from their perspective, they put their own Christian identity at risk'. (4)

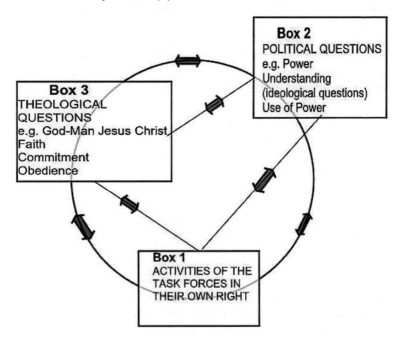

from *Concerning Theological Reflection* by David Jenkins (amended)

Using the Hermeneutic Cycle

The next development was the increasing use of the Hermeneutic (or Pastoral) cycle. David Jenkins had published a version of the cycle in a paper published in 1971 in WCC Study Encounter. (5) This emerged from his work as the Director of the World Council of Churches Humanum Programme. He linked ideas arising from a number of task groups (who were looking at the role of Christians in situations where our common humanity was threatened and should be protected) to theological questions and political questions by circles moving both clockwise and anti-clockwise. Quite soon the model was simplified and the process moved from Box 1 to 2 to 3 and usually drawn clockwise.

At that time IM used three words to explain their work as 'participation, reflection, and evaluation' enshrined in the document *Guidelines on the Task, Organisation, Appointments and Continuity of Industrial Mission.* (6) See also Chapter 1 reference (18). These fitted well into the Hermeneutic Cycle.

The Participation, Reflection and Evaluation model

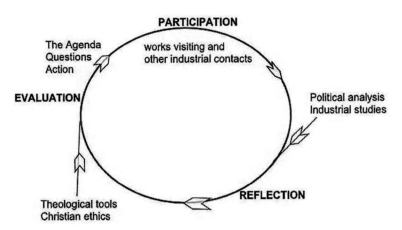

Ian Fraser creates a usable model

The breakthrough in IM's use of the Hermeneutic Cycle came in June 1979 when Ian Fraser, at that time Dean of Mission at the Selly Oak Colleges, ran a five-day course for IM staff. (7) They took as a case study the work of the Lucas Aerospace Shop

Stewards who, faced with a reduction in orders for the company's military products, had produced an *Alternative company strategy for making socially useful products*. This was a significant choice of material as it dealt with the potential for trades unions to influence company policy beyond wages and conditions. The study group's work was tested on the last day when their reflections and proposals for action were presented to representatives of the company and the trades unions. The visitors agreed that the analysis of their situation had been useful, that some creative thinking had been done, although the applications raised more questions than solutions.

Ian Fraser had made the model more usable when he proposed using two key questions in the Analysis phase, and brainstorming in the Reflection phase. Thus the basic model for using the Hermeneutic Cycle in IM was set out in five steps:

---

1 Experience
    Tell the story of the situation
2 Analysis
    Identify the most significant themes in the situation
3 For each theme list:
    a the Powers at work
    b the major Human consequences
4 Reflection
    Identify relevant Biblical and theological resources
    a for each Power
    b for each Human consequence
5 Response
    Apply the relevant Biblical and theological resources to the original situation.

First in the analysis step, the situation is broken down into <u>themes</u> – embodying the understanding that theology is best thought of as a narrative rather than a theory. Secondly, in the political analysis of the situation, the Fraser model introduced two specific questions about each theme, or at least those themes chosen for detailed study.

    What are the powers at work?
    What are the effects on people (stress all the people affected)?

Those are powerful tools. 'Powers' has meaning both in the daily papers and in Paul's theology: 'Our struggle is not against enemies of flesh and blood but against the rulers, (principalities and powers in the AV) against the cosmic powers of this present darkness' (Ephesians 6v12). Principalities and Powers – over whom the Cosmic Christ rules 'whether thrones or dominions or powers' (Colossians 1v16). This provides a way of connecting with the Bible and with Christian traditions.

'Effects on People' is, for Christians, the bottom line – not profit and loss; the measure of how humanity is affirmed or diminished giving a bridge to measuring humanity against the stature of Christ. 'Whatever you did to one of these least of these you did to me' (Matthew 25v40).

Used in this way the Hermeneutic circle helps to correlate aspects of the situation as analysed to specific parts of the Christian tradition in bible, liturgy and church practice – which are the deposits of earlier generations of Christians correlating their human existence with divine revelation. From the standpoint of those relevant parts of the tradition the situation is re-examined, interrogated from a different position, leading to alternative solutions. In 1980 Ian Fraser published his explanation of the need for such a method and its justification in *Reinventing Theology as the People's Work*. (8)

The Fraser model in use

Industrial Mission in Hertfordshire and Bedfordshire ran two one-day conferences for lay people in May 1981, to examine the model's value for lay people. Again they used a case study dealing with an industrial relations situation, showing IM's intense interest in this field at the time. Whilst it revealed some limitations arising out of gaps in the participants' biblical knowledge these conferences produced relevant and challenging insights. In 1984 Industrial Mission in South Yorkshire began using the model in their annual summer courses for theological students. As each year's cohort focussed on different issues this provided a wide-ranging test of the method. In a year when mass redundancies were occurring students used the model to respond to experiences during the course and summed up their findings thus:

We looked for ways in which the individual's personal usefulness and worth could be affirmed in ways other than through traditional employment. We also noted that this sense of worth was often physically, socially or economically denied in much local employment in steel and other heavy industries. We concluded that jobs were inherently valuable and many of the group would join public protest against plant closures.

The full-scale model proved to be a useful in teaching and in project work. It was incorporated into the IMA Induction Course for new IM staff. Mike West reviewed six years' experience of the Course in his paper in *Industrial Mission in a Changing World.* (9) He gives some examples of biblical sources which were used in a study of cost cutting in a company's drive for efficiency:

Falsifying scales in Amos, the unjust steward, making bricks without straw, Naboth's Vineyard, Paul and the silversmiths.

And in dealing with people's insecurity as a company sought savings:

Sing us the songs of Zion in Babylon, Peter walking (or rather not walking) on the water, early church meetings behind closed doors.

These examples demonstrate the creative use of biblical sources, used only after critical study of their original context. They also demonstrate Ronald Preston's criticism of the Hermeneutic cycle, 'it all depends on which Biblical material is held to be relevant'. (10)

It should be noted that these explorations into Hermeneutics all took place before the subject was easily accessible in Britain. Laurie Green's valuable book *Let's do Theology* (11) was not published until 1990 and the more comprehensive review by Paul Ballard and John Pritchard (12) until 1996. These focussed on pastoral care in parochial situations rather than public, industrial situations. The earlier works in which the notion of 'Doing Theology' appeared (13) came from Latin American and largely Liberation theology oriented authors. IM can rightly claim that its serious attempts to 'do theology' were innovative and relevant to the task of 'informing and energising the people of God for faithful lives'.

The Theological Grid
The full-scale Fraser model proved to be a useful tool in teaching and in project work. Chaplains did use modified versions almost on

the hoof but it was too complex for general use. Something simpler was called for.

Mike West and Malcolm Brown developed this model for use in the IMA Induction Course for new Industrial Mission staff. This simple model analyses a situation in ways that help to make connections to the Christian traditions. It is generated by combining two analytical tools which then produce nine components (or boxes) in each of which it may be possible to see some connections with Christian traditions, to 'do theology'.

Mission in three modes or activities

Mission activity can be analysed into three modes, using a model proposed by Harvey Cox in *The Secular City* (14), and based upon Luke 4vv18-19:

> *The Spirit of the Lord is upon me because he has anointed me to preach good news to the poor. He has sent me to proclaim release to the captives and recovery of sight to the blind, to set at liberty those who are oppressed, to proclaim the acceptable year of the Lord.*

The three modes are:

a) Proclamation – exposing what God is doing; with a message of judgment and hope, in specific terms, related to specific situations, usually in non-religious language.
b) Healing – serving the weak and injured; both directly and by working for social structures which promote human development, loving relationships and responsible use of the earth's resources.
c) Being the new Community – making visible the 'new community of new men and women'; living as though the Kingdom had come, on a small scale: acted parables.

Some activities contain elements of all three modes, though one usually dominates.

Mission on three levels

This way of sub-dividing the missionary task sociologically, which is particularly appropriate to people at work, was developed by South

London Industrial Mission who called it 'Three Gear Mission' (by analogy with the gears of a car).

First Level (Personal) – as an individual, 'the neighbour' in face to face relationships or in very small groups, e.g. the family, independent of status, role, etc. Often this has been the only aspect of life that has been given a Christian dimension.

Second Level (Institutional) – affecting the behaviour and policy of departments and smaller companies, trade unions or professional groups. How to be a Christian engineer, shop steward or shareholder.

Third Level (National/Global) – affecting the behaviour and policy of the largest companies, Governments and international bodies. How to be a Christian citizen (and for the few) Prime Minister or Chief Executive.

All three levels are needed to understand and tackle any major issue, though each individual will have particular pressures and opportunities in one level more than the others. These two ways of analyzing a situation, mission in three modes and on three levels, create a nine box grid.

MODE LEVEL	Proclamation What to say?	Healing Who to support?	Being the New Community
1st level Personal			
2nd level Institutional			
3rd level National/ Global			

This technique proved to be usable in a wide range of situations. This example was produced by the Chaplain to Cambridge Science

Park, to help him focus his efforts in work with a complex mixture of small companies.

MODE LEVEL	Proclamation What to say?	Healing Who to support?	Being the New Community
1st level Personal	Individuals connecting Faith and Work	One-to-one Counselling	A cross level/multi company Christian cell
2nd level Institutional	Affirming values in e.g. ISO 9000 Investors in People.	Talking to Staff Associations, negotiations about welfare issues etc.	Invite Companies to exhibit at an Industrial Harvest Festival
3rd level National/ Global	Chaplain's voice in the Boardroom	Affirming recycling projects	Contact with Science Parks in Europe

A deductive model

Although IM staff found inductive theological models useful for their collective thinking they also used deductive models where appropriate. To be able to correlate appropriate texts to the studied situation assumes a wide knowledge of the bible and Christian history. Where this could not be assumed, for example when reporting to church groups on IM work, and particularly when working with lay people on their responsibilities in their work lives other models were necessary. These groups contained people with a wide variety of employment situations and mixed understandings of the problems they faced. With them the early stages of inductive processes were difficult. But they did share a broad understanding of Christian principles, and were motivated to make better decisions. When Christians disagree about what is the best course of action in a situation it is often because they are giving different weights to these principles. It is hard to see the problem from every angle at the same time.

Peter Cope and Chris Gilbert, at that time members of the Black Country Urban Industrial Mission team, produced a short workbook for use with lay and clergy groups. (15) They began with a long list of *Christian Moral Perspectives (MP)* but in order to make the model manageable these were distilled to six.

MP1   *The world and all that is in it is created and redeemed by God – and therefore is good.*

MP2   *The value and dignity of human life.*

MP3   *The unity of the Human Family in God.*

MP4   *Human responsibility to promote love and justice, giving priority to the poor, and to care for God's creation.*

MP5   *Human vocation as God given.*

MP6   *Human Limitations and Sinfulness.*

To these six it was found necessary to add a further MP to deal with international conflicts leading to wars.

MP7   *The justification for using military force to settle international disputes.*

The biblical and theological bases of each of these Moral Perspectives are outlined. The workbook outlines a process of evaluating possible solutions and outcomes against every Moral Perspective as if each in turn were the only or most weighty principle. It clearly demonstrates how widely different conclusions can be reached by giving each Perspective more weight than the others. These six evaluations are then combined to seek an optimum solution. The workbook gives three worked examples: a parish dealing with a beautiful but redundant church, a company whose chimney is polluting the neighbourhood, and the First Iraq war.

After using the model in the case study on pollution caused by a factory the conclusions were summarised thus:

> *A possible Christian judgement of this issue would be to recognise and support the moral purpose of the company in manufacturing good products which meet human need, and providing employment and income for local people. However the company was clearly neglecting their responsibility to the community and to care for the environment. They should therefore have taken steps to clean up the air pollution caused by their operation as soon as they could afford it after this problem became known. To prevent*

this happening in similar situations in the future the law on industrial pollution may need to be strengthened, and the way in which it is enforced by local authorities.

In the case of the redundant church there were five possible solutions. All but Option 5 involved selling the church building and using the income for local church purposes. The alternative uses would have different sale values and different effects on the community:

Op 1 sell the church to the highest bidder for commercial use.
Op 2 sell for use as a Mosque.
Op 3 sell for use as a Community Centre – at a much lower price.
Op 4 sell to a Housing Association to create Sheltered Housing.
Op 5 seek grants to restore the church for public worship.

Each Option was scored against each Moral Perspective thus:

A Preferred Option   P
A Possible Option   OK
Ruled Out.   X

These are then fed into a matrix thus:

	Op 1	Op 2	Op 3	Op 4	Op5
MP 1	X	OK	OK	OK	P
MP 2	OK	OK	P	OK	OK
MP 3	OK	P	OK	OK	X
MP 4	OK	OK	P	P	X
MP 5	P	OK	P	OK	OK
MP 6	OK	OK	P	OK	OK
Results	1 P 4 OK	1 P 5 OK	4 P 2 OK	1 P 5 OK	1 P 3 OK

This does not deliver an unarguably best course of action but it focusses attention on Option 3, and Options 2 and 4 are also worth closer study.

Participants using this and other methods developed by IM recognised the similarity with decision making systems they might be using in their working life. This in itself helped to make the bridge between their Christian beliefs and the problems faced in work.

The authors conclude:

> It is no ethical blueprint! However those who use this method to solve problems and make moral decisions can at least be confident that they are doing so on clear Christian grounds, even if their own understanding of those grounds will inevitably differ. Using this method will not necessarily produce agreement amongst Christians on the way to solve issues, but the important thing is that we have put our faith to work on these issues in the best way we know how.

Theology as a core skill

IM's commitment to the importance of theology was clearly stated in the document *Core Skills for Workplace Chaplains* produced by the IMA Training Working Party in 2001, that alongside economic, practical, pastoral and prophetic skills every chaplain also needed to have theological skills:

> This involves showing that I understand why I undertake workplace visiting. I can do this by:
> a) Describing, in explicitly theological terms, why I undertake workplace visiting with particular reference to the theology of mission and evangelism;
> b) Explaining, in terms understandable in any local church why I undertake workplace visiting;
> c) Explaining what I am doing in the workplace to people of all faiths and none.

Development of relevant Christian ethics

In this section we consider four issues in which IM developed an ethical stance: the nature of the company, the role of trades unions, humanising the redundancy experience and the search for equality in employment.

The nature of the company – a unitary or pluralistic system?

A major perspective applied to a wide variety of situations grew from the biblical image of the body. Through their more or less equal relations with people at all levels chaplains were often more aware of what held them together than was voiced by individuals in different parts of the enterprise. Certain departments would see themselves at the centre of the business, held back even opposed by others. Chaplains used the biblical metaphor of the body to raise questions about the contributions of different work groups to the total purpose of the enterprise. Whilst almost all workplace chaplaincy in the private sector was in traditionally structured companies there was considerable interest in alternatives. IM's work in steel during the period when the industry was nationalised brought chaplains into contact with the elected Worker Directors. Chaplains were also aware of more radical models in the growing number of worker co-operatives. Frank Scuffham, a member of the Peterborough IM team was for a time the Community Director of one of the best known co-operatives, The Scott Bader Commonwealth. The exchange programmes between UK and West Germany exposed participants to the German Co-determination model. Greater Manchester Industrial Mission worked with their German counterparts to produce a substantial report comparing and contrasting British and German systems. (16) When the Donovan Commission rejected the creation of Worker Directors or Works Councils on the German model in all large British companies many in IM were disappointed. (17)

Whilst affirming the company as a single human and morally responsible community chaplains rejected the 'team model' of the enterprise in which owners and managers sought to impose their understanding of the company on everyone, and classed other positions as 'disloyal' or 'trouble making'. Alan Fox, an academic sociologist and popular speaker at several IM meetings and conferences in the 1970s, called this view 'the unitary frame of reference', in which there is one focus of loyalty and one source of authority. (18) In this chaplains also drew on the body image, which is critical of those who claim their standpoint is the only legitimate position. Here chaplains referred to St Paul's comparison of dissention in the Corinthian church to the ear saying 'because I am not an eye I am not part of the body' (1 Corinthians 12v16). Chaplains found a role in helping to interpret one part of a company to others, not by representing the other's views but asking people to imagine what the situation might look like from another's standpoint. Using the body image they looked for ways in which different standpoints could be regarded as legitimate. In this they also followed Fox's identification of the industrial enterprise as a 'pluralistic frame of reference' containing many related but separate interests and objectives which must be maintained in some kind of equilibrium. (See reference above)

A positive view of the roles and responsibilities of trades unions.

Experiencing the working life of manual and staff workers led IM staff to recognise the legitimacy of their discontents and to adopt a positive attitude to the role of trades unions. Good relations were usually established with elected shop floor trade union representatives (often but not always called shop stewards) and in many areas with local full time officials. With these activists there was the possibility of a lively debate about both company problems and wider issues. IM staff were welcome visitors to Trades Union branch and Trades Union Conference meetings; many took out trade union membership long before it became an issue for all ministers. Here they were drawing on the Christian Social Ethics tradition developed in the first half of the twentieth century, in which the right to form and belong to a trade union had been established. In 1977 the Church of England Industrial Committee published its study of the Closed Shop, (an examination of what was then a politically contentious issue). It included the statement that 'Trades Unions are a legitimate means by which working people can be both protected and represented at their place of work'. (19) The 1958 Lambeth Conference called upon laypeople as part of their Christian service to play a responsible role in their trades union. This was put more strongly by the Roman Catholic Bishops of England and Wales in 1988 who spoke of the 'right of workers to be represented by their trades union'.

However these opinions of academics and church leaders seem not to have penetrated the church at large. Ronald Preston wrote in 1986: 'Individual Christians have made striking contributions to the labour movement but the churches have not yet come to terms with the phenomenon of the industrial worker'. (20) As IM's general sympathy with the role of trades unions was not widely held in the church it may have been one of the reasons why it was seen as 'left wing'. IM never took an uncritical stance on trades union rights and policies but did support the rights of trades unions to organise and represent workers. In situations where these were opposed by management it could create difficulties for IM.

The issue can be clearly seen in this example. As a result of the Industrial Relations Act 1971 Kodak agreed to recognise its in-house Workers' Representative Committee as a Trade Union, but denied recognition rights to TUC affiliated unions. In 1973 this led to a strike by the union Association of Cinematograph, Television and Allied Technicians (ACTT). The chaplain to the Hemel Hempstead plant, Antony Dalling argued that workers not only had the right to be represented but also to choose which union. The IM in Hertfordshire and Bedfordshire team issued a statement to this effect but without consulting the chaplain from the London IM team in the company's Harrow factory. Kodak complained to the Bishop of St Albans and threatened to end the chaplaincy. Canon Eric James on behalf of the Bishop negotiated a settlement. The affair demonstrated the risks inherent in public stances, and the need for proper consultation between teams dealing with the same employer on different sites. (21)

As British companies became incorporated into international enterprises IM teams saw that trades unions needed to develop their thinking and practice to respond effectively. The World Council of Churches had studied transnational corporations (TNCs) at its General Assembly meeting in Nairobi in 1975. They called upon member churches to 'continue research and develop documentation on the role of TNCs in order to enable people to participate in the shaping of a new economic order'. Their perspective was shaped by churches in the Third World who held that 'TNCs in league with oppressive regimes distort and exploit the economies of poor nations'. (22) The European Contact Group on Church and Industry (ECG) took up the issue and in 1976 recommended that 'IM teams help Trades Unions study to understand the multinational nature of the companies they worked with, and where possible to use IM contacts to meet their counterparts in other countries'. (23)

This had already been achieved through one UK-Germany exchange programme. In 1972 the IM team in Russelsheim, headquarters of General Motors German subsidiary Opel made contact with IM in Hertfordshire and Bedfordshire, which had a long established chaplaincy in the Vauxhall plants. This led to a series of exchange visits, informal at first, between plant-level trades union officials in the two companies. ECG contributed to the travel costs of the Vauxhall participants, whilst the Opel Works Council education funds supported their part of the programme. Vauxhall management strongly expressed their disapproval to the chaplain, but made no threats to interfere or suspend the chaplaincy. At the beginning the project was wholly owned by the IM team, with unofficial trades union participation. It gradually became owned by the Vauxhall Trades Unions, who made it official policy in 1976, and created official channels and ultimately a General Motors European Trades Union Council. The foundation for understanding and trust between the two very different trades union systems was created by those exchanges. Further details are given in Chapter 5.

Humanising the experience of redundancy
The rapid increase in mass redundancies in the mid 1970s called for a response by IM teams based on their solidarity with workers whom they had known through plant visiting. Faced with the hurt and confusion experienced by workers who were being thrown out of work in the heavy industries in their area, an experience compared with bereavement, Newport and Gwent IM convened a small group of managers, trades union officials and civil servants. In 1975 they published a booklet *Redundant? a personal survival kit.* (24) It contained information and advice covering the period from when redundancies are first announced, through the last days in employment into the first weeks of unemployment. It began 'Remember that being made redundant is not your fault; you do not need to feel ashamed about it'. As much of the information was changing rapidly it was produced in a loose-leaf format. The first edition was of 100 copies, as many as the IM

funds would support. A second printing carried messages of support from leaders of the Confederation of British Industry (CBI) and the Trades Union Congress (TUC). There were even rumours that the Department of Employment might subsidise large numbers. Later the Department did produce information leaflets but these lacked the personal and compassionate tone of the original. At 40 pages long and costing 60p it was clearly not appropriate for mass circulation so many IM teams created their own shorter versions covering the same questions, usually on four A5 pages. These were not only given away freely in companies where chaplains operated, they were sold to other local firms with mass redundancies. In 1979 the Newport and Gwent IM produced 4000 copies of *Redundancy – the last option*, a professionally printed report focussed on company policy. This is a significant example of the way in which IM moved from pastoral concern for individuals hurt by economic change to structural and political issues for companies and government.

Advice and information was an inadequate response to some of these situations. Many teams came to the conclusion that redundancies should be opposed, if only to test the argument that they were the only viable policy. 'It is impossible not to stand with workers we know as they protest their redundancy'. Mention was made in Chapter 1 of the public enquiry in 1973 into the proposed closure of the Copenacre Naval Base by the Bristol team. When Scottish steel workers marched to London to protest the first wave of closures in their industry Scottish chaplains accompanied them, and used their contacts in England to organise practical and political welcome in the towns they passed through. The two People's Marches for Jobs (1981 and 1983) attracted wider church support including many IM staff. A photograph of the Bishop of Doncaster welcoming marchers to the town, taken by a chaplain, featured on the front page of the *Morning Star*. IM's wide ranging involvement in schemes for unemployed people was outlined in Chapter 1.

The search for equality in employment

The fourth ethical issue which frequently appeared in Doing Theology exercises was that of equality, or rather the inequalities in the workplace measured against the belief that all are equal before God. This was, or ought to have been a two-edged sword, given that

IM as an employer and the churches more generally were poor examples of equal opportunities practice. The issue was first discussed in the Churches Consortium on Industrial Mission in October 1978. It called upon teams to take more seriously the situation of women workers in the companies they visited, and at the same time for the churches to open up all IM posts equally to women and men, and to ordained and lay people. In the survey carried out for *Industrial Mission – an Appraisal* in 1986 only 34 of the 403 posts (full-, half- and part-time) were filled by women, and a small but uncounted number of black chaplains. (25) This probably under represents the proportion of full-time posts held by women, certainly a higher proportion than in the church at large at that time.

IM's longest established work was in steel, coal and engineering, all situations of 'men's work' with its associated culture. One of the motivations within the churches for sending chaplains into industry was to reach working class men who were largely absent from their congregations. With this background it is easy to see why IM found it as hard as any other part of the church to challenge the inequalities experienced by women. When the Church of England report on women's experience of discrimination and low pay at work, *All that is unseen* (26) was reviewed by its Industrial Committee, it concluded that IM like the rest of the church still had much room for improvement.

The IMA created a Women's and Men's Network in February 1980, after some sharp discussion at the National Conference. The Network greatly helped its members to come to terms with the deep cultural roots of gender inequality, and helped to raise those questions within teams. Despite the clearly stated commitment of IM teams and personnel to equality there were few programmes to highlight the issue, to challenge employers and trades unions or to support individuals suffering discrimination. In 1992 Anne Morris, a member of Greater Manchester IM in her MA thesis on *Women and Industrial Mission – a critical study* portrayed IM in a 'fairly negative light.' She surveyed women engaged in IM and concluded that 'the structures and patterns of work in IM were only just beginning to adjust to the very substantial changes in women's labour'. (27)

However, the appointment of Olwen Smith to be Team leader of one of the largest teams – the Black Country Urban Industrial Mission(BCUIM) – in 1994 demonstrated that Industrial Mission was able to offer equal opportunity to women candidates. Under her leadership, BCUIM developed creative engagement on behalf of the churches with economic development work over the whole Black Country area.

The politicised issue of race inequality in most workplaces in the 1970s and 80s and was also hard to handle whilst preserving IM's independence. In 1989 South London Industrial Mission appointed Guyanan born Ray Singh to develop a programme for racial justice, both within that team and more widely through the IMA. It was 1997 before questions of the employment of people with disabilities began to be discussed within the IMA. After that date most issues of *IMAgenda* carried articles dealing with aspects of the struggle for equality in employment. Perhaps the relatively weak action by IM on equality issues indicates the way that the informal nature of chaplaincy arrangements with its pastoral image inhibited taking effective action on such social and therefore political issues.

Theology Development Group

In the 1970s there was a growing feeling that if the kind of theological thinking produced for the 1971 IMA Conference in IM was to develop it needed both concentrated work and wider publicity. For this purpose the IMA Theology Development Group was formed in 1975. It aimed to fill a gap left by the deaths of Temple, Tawney and Oldham, whose writings had provided high level theological thinking relevant to those grappling with industrial, economic and political issues. There was also a realisation that theological thinking in Asia, Africa and elsewhere in Europe was challenging the British model of Christian social teaching. The group met for two or three 30-hour residential conferences each year between 1975 and 1990. Members wrote papers which were critically reviewed by the Group. Some of these emerged as a series of booklets published by the William Temple Foundation. (See the appendix to this chapter)

From the mid 1980s the TDG had asked itself questions about its value and purpose. Teams were constantly finding new tasks in responding to unemployment and participating in local economic regeneration, often with reduced resources. The cost in time and money to attend TDG meetings became harder to justify. Teaching Doing Theology still had a major place in the IMA Induction Course programme. Teams wrestling with the questions of 'what to say' and 'what to do' in the rapidly changing industrial world were as theologically rooted as ever. When *IMAgenda* replaced the *IMA Newsletter* in 1995 its policy was to include articles on both theology and spirituality in most issues. But the impetus provided by the TDG was lost.

Despite the conflicting pressures of demand and resources IM continued to earn this tribute from Peter Selby (then Bishop of Kingston) in the Report *Industrial Mission – an Appraisal* :

> *Industrial Mission has been from the beginning an extended seminar in applied theology, conducted in an unfamiliar setting (the workplace) and with no guaranteed audience. In the process of clarifying its own mission it has raised issues about the mission of the whole Church in the world.* (28)

Notes and references to this chapter

1. H Richard Niebuhr, *Christ and Culture,* Torchbooks (1951).
2. Peter Berger, *A Rumor of Angels,* Anchor at Random House (1970).
3. IMA Conference 1971 duplicated papers.
4. Margaret Kane, *Characteristics of Industrial Mission's Theology* in *Thinking in Practice; Working Papers from Industrial Mission No 3*; William Temple Foundation for the TDG (1980) p 23.
5. David Jenkins, *Concerning Theological Reflection,* in Study Encounter SE/11; Vol VII/No 3, World Council of Churches (1971).
6. *Guidelines on the Task, Organisation, Appointments and Continuity of Industrial Mission,* Churches Consortium on Industrial Mission (1977). It states, 'Industrial Mission works for the reordering of the relationships, methods and goals of industry and commerce, in the light of the Christian hope for justice and community, and through the process of participation, reflection and evaluation'.
7. *IMA Newsletter,* January 1980.

8. Ian M Fraser, *Reinventing Theology as the People's Work,* Wild Goose revised edition (1988) p 73ff.
9. Mike West, *Doing Theology – a Model examined;* in *Industrial Mission in a Changing world,* edited by John W Rogerson, Sheffield Academic Press (1996).
10. Private correspondence from Professor Ronald Preston.
11. Laurie Green, *Let's do Theology – a Pastoral Cycle Resource Book,* Mowbrays (1990).
12. Paul Ballard and John Pritchard, *Practical Theology in Action,* SPCK (1996).
13. Usefully summarised in Stephen B Bevans, *Models of Contextual Theology,* Orbis (1997) especially Chapter 6 'The Praxis Model'.
14. Harvey Cox, *The Secular City,* SCMP (1966) p 125ff.
15. *The Incredible Flying Machine – a way of making Christian decisions,* by Peter Cope and Christine Gilbert; published by the Black Country Urban Industrial Mission (1992). The authors state that 'the model might look ramshackle at first, rather like an early aeroplane, but it might fly!' A version was later published as an Audenshaw Paper.
16. *Industrial Democracy: ways forward in Britain and West Germany,*Anglo German Foundation for the Study of Industrial Society (1979).
17. *The Report of the Royal Commission on Trade Unions and Employers Associations chaired by Lord Donovan;* paragraph 1105, HMSO (1968).
18. Alan Fox, *Industrial Sociology and Industrial Relations,* Donovan Commission Research Paper No 3 HMSO (1966) pp 2 – 14.
19. *Understanding Closed Shops,* Publishing for the General Synod18. Board for Social Responsibility, CIO (1977) p 28.
20. Ronald Preston, in *A New Dictionary of Christian Ethics,* article on Labour Movements, SCMP (1986). The article *Trade Unions* by the same author does not debate the legitimacy of Trades Unions but only their potential role in management and the closed shop.
21. *Runcie: on Reflection,* edited S Platten, Canterbury Press (2002) article by Eric James. Note that the two authors of this book found themselves on different sides in this situation(!), as Peter Cope was chaplain at Kodak Harrow, whilst Mike West was Dalling's senior colleague in the Herts and Beds IM team.

22. *Breaking Barriers Nairobi 1975,* edited by D M Paton; Section VI; Resolution 78; SPCK for the World Council of Churches (1976). The WCC like the United Nations preferred to refer to Transnational Companies. In Europe the term Multinational Companies was used at first, but later fell into the UN usage.

23. *Multinational Companies – A Working Document,* European Contact Group on Church and Industry (1976).

24. *Redundant? a Personal Survival Kit,* Newport and Gwent Industrial 24. Mission (1975).

25. *Industrial Mission - an Appraisal,* (see reference above) p 122.

26. *All that is Unseen,* CIO (1986).

27. *IMA Newsletter,* February 1992.

28. *Industrial Mission - an Appraisal,* (see reference above) p 49.

Appendix

Working Papers from Industrial Mission

ONE *Theology and Politics* (1978) 58 pp

Five papers on the developing political context of IM in Britain; Christian-Marxist dialogue, inequality, the National Front, Christians and the Labour movement; together with an introduction to the series by John Atherton, the Secretary of the TDG.

TWO *The End of Work – papers on Theology and Technological Change* (1980) 88 pp

Seven papers dealing with the technological, educational, employment social issues arising from the introduction of microelectronics. The introductory article by John Atherton gives details of the TDG's origins and programmes.

THREE *Thinking in Practice: Theology and Industrial Mission,* (1980) 108pp

Nine papers. Three covered general issues: the early influences on IM (Michael Atkinson), the characteristics of IM Theology (Margaret Kane) and the contribution of theology to IM (John Atherton). The others were theological explorations of current issues: British Steel's partnership contract, industrial relations, wage differentials, the changing nature of work, organisation size, and young unemployed people.

FOUR *Spirituality and Necessity* (1982) 50 pp.

In his Editor's introduction Rodney Ward rejects the notion that spirituality is only about religious experience or an escape from the realities of the everyday. In industrial mission spirituality is seen 'in terms of the total life environment, including church, work, politics, technology and the secular, as the overarching mode of experience'.

FIVE *Changing Industrial Mission – models and hopes* (1983) 86 pp

Introduction by John Rogan (who worked in Sheffield 1950 – 1962) described the changes in IM over 40 years. Five essays outlining the work in situations as diverse as the Port of London and the Greater Manchester conurbation; with two concluding reflections on the role of lay people and IM strategy and resources.

All were lithographed from typed text in an A5 booklet.

Ted Wickham in Firth Vickers Steels, Sheffield mid 1950s

Margaret Kane in Firth Brown Special Steel works, Sheffield circa 1962

Mike West in Hawker Siddeley Aviation Hatfield June 1977

Peter Cope in Brockhouse Forgings Ltd, West Bromwich 1993

Lynn Jameson with Turgut Turna owner of Demure in MetroCentre Gateshead 2010.

Andrew Jolly on the Total Manifold Compression Platform 173 Km north of Aberdeen. Andrew was awarded the MBE for his work in 2009 and sadly died in 2010.

Mike Fox at GKN Land Systems 28 April 2011
With two shop stewards, planting a tree to mark Workers'
Memorial Day.

Opel Trades Unionists visiting Vauxhall Motors Luton; September
1974.

Yorkshire and Portuguese Homeworkers during a conference in Leeds brought together by the West Yorkshire Homeworkers Group 1991.
Dian Leppington third from right

Sheffield Industrial Mission Theological Students Summer School – visiting Thurnscoe Colliery June 1987

Industrial Mission Association Induction Course
Training visit to Vauxhall Motors January 1999.

Redundancy – The Last Option booklet published by Newport and
Gwent Industrial Mission 1979

CHAPTER FOUR

The Method of Mission in the Workplace

British Industrial Mission was, and is, a heroic pioneering movement. Chaplains have gained entry into many of the principal industries. One of the great strengths is still the regular visiting of people while they are at work. Arising from this fundamental method of working has developed the study of a wide range of issues. There has been an honest exploration of major practices and values in the light of Christian faith.

Malcolm Grundy, *An Unholy Conspiracy*, Canterbury Press, Norwich (1992) p 73

Introduction

The story of the development of industrial mission in Britain has been told, at least in outline. The theological context in which it grew, and some of the great twentieth-century theological figures which influenced its development, have been described. The way in which industrial mission practitioners worked with others to create practical theological and ethical models for immediate application to current workplace situations, was outlined in the last chapter. But how was the work actually done? How were the priorities set, the workplaces chosen, and access negotiated? What were the practical aims and how were the results assessed? The following two chapters attempt to answer these questions, first in respect of workplace chaplaincy in this chapter, and secondly examining all manner of industrial mission projects beyond the workplace in Chapter 5.

Two different models for workplace visiting

This chapter is about the theory and practice of workplace chaplaincy, which is how industrial mission began and has always been an important part of it – but never the whole of it. Workplace chaplaincy provided the context and structure for the contact between representatives of the Church and the many thousands who had lost contact with this institution which purported to care for them in the name of Jesus Christ. There were at least two different models for this work.

Malcolm Torry in his recent book on the history of workplace chaplaincy (1) usefully describes the original aims and development of the work in South London and Sheffield in successive chapters. We have already noted in Chapter 1 how, in 1940, Cuthbert Bardsley began his ministry with the employees at Siemens in Woolwich on the same pastoral lines as a forces chaplain or 'padre'. When Colin Cuttell joined him in 1944 as an industrial missioner he continued in the traditional pastoral model of caring for individuals and their families in Christ's name, and as the work expanded in the 1950s other chaplains followed Cuttell's example. (2)

In contrast, Ted Wickham in Sheffield, whilst anxious to meet everyone at Firth Vickers (3), or wherever else he might be visiting, **did not** have as his main objective doing pastoral work with individual employees. He certainly did not hold any religious services in workplaces. He was aiming to create a 'web of personal relationships', and particularly with 'the representative persons who man the great industries'. (4) Rather than to operate within a company as a traditional parish priest would work within his parish and community, Wickham wanted to make a contribution to the whole life and direction of that company. As he put it later: 'Industrial Mission is just one attempt to "influence the influences" in the industrial context'. (5) He also wanted to have real dialogue with people estranged from the Church about the meaning of the world in which they lived, seeing God's activity in it, and the relevance of the Christian gospel – and so he frequently arranged 'snap-break meetings', as we have seen. (6) These meetings were also the entry-point by which people were given the opportunity to think about the issues more deeply at further meetings held outside work, to become members of a regular worshipping group, and even take responsibility for the future development of this work. (7)

So the work in South London and in Sheffield in their early years would have appeared fairly different – the former a pastoral model, and the latter a theological and political dialogue approach. However, as the years went by, and there was some contact between these different mission projects, one cannot help wondering whether these differences slowly became less significant. Both projects were motivated by an urgent desire to present the relevance of the Christian gospel to people in the twentieth century, most of whom had been largely estranged from it, and had experienced tremendous difficulty, dislocation and even suffering through the Second World War. Arguably the Sheffield approach took that estrangement more seriously, and therefore deliberately tried to engage people on an intellectual level, and to avoid any element of traditional evangelism.

One very practical difference between the traditional pastoral one of South London, and the more strategic approach in Sheffield was the pressure on the industrial missioner as he or she tried to deal with scores of people in the course of a day's work in the large workplaces in which this work began. Part of Wickham's vision from the beginning was that lay people should play a major role in leading this work, and in assisting chaplains wherever possible. It is interesting that in 1957 Cuttell appointed 'keymen' in many of the places in which he or other chaplains visited, to encourage and recruit more lay members for 'South London Industrial Mission' (SLIM) as it became in 1955; some keymen convened groups, or distributed *Over the Bridge* (the Cathedral magazine), or let the chaplain know of anyone who needed pastoral care.

The personal qualities which industrial mission practitioners – the openness to everyone, the discipline and perseverance, and not least the courage to overcome suspicion and alienation which in some cases might have very long and deep roots, should not be under-estimated. Some chaplains have admitted to driving into the car park at an established workplace chaplaincy, and struggling for a long time to decide whether or not to enter the factory, or simply to drive away. Brian Cordingley (8) tells a true story about one of his colleagues, Tim Baynes and a group of railway platelayers near Manchester Piccadilly station.

They had a cabin half a mile up the track. Tim went to visit them at breakfast time once a month. For the first three or four visits, when he arrived they all lifted their newspapers in front of their faces and read them like that until, after an interminable period of silence, he left. It was on the third or fourth visit that one of them said: "I reckon you must believe in what you're doing to come here like this." That broke the ice, and Tim got on fine with the platelayers thereafter.

Margaret Halsey describes crossing 'boundaries of culture' in her weekly visits as chaplain to a Rotherham steelworks. That task would often begin with the exchange: 'Afternoon, yer Grace'. 'Afternoon, comrade.' She immediately explains that she had no aspirations to that title, but admits that this humour was one of the bonuses of the job. (9) Most importantly, of course, it demonstrated that she had successfully crossed the cultural boundary and had been accepted by those she was visiting.

Building relationships with people was and is the key task of workplace chaplains, and in this task conversation is an essential tool. Chaplains have to design visiting strategies to enable serial conversations with perhaps a large number of people to take place on a reasonably regular basis, so that understanding and awareness can be built up over time (see below for details in 'Developing a Plan'). Other features of the work environment and the company could provide formidable challenges to a workplace chaplain. Excessive noise from the production process (100 decibels or more) obviously makes conversation very difficult – although a degree of noise often provides some privacy in talking to individuals. Experience showed that some privacy in conversation with a chaplain was important for people – which is probably the reason that many chaplains have found visiting large open-plan offices quite difficult. The prevailing culture in a company was also important: workplace chaplaincy could operate successfully in companies in which open and critical conversations about the company – its products, policies, wage-levels and future – could take place without either the employee or the chaplain being regarded as disloyal or subversive.

In terms of how the results of a particular day's workplace visiting could be assessed, apart from structured activities such as the Sheffield 'meetings' (and for others, see later in this chapter), chaplains would often measure this by the number of quality, in-depth conversations they managed to have. These might well begin with a recent event or a current issue in the company, but they might also begin with a situation in that person's life, or even with an important issue raised in the media. Mention might well be made of a biblical story or text, and very likely the meaning of values such as love, justice, truth, goodness or community in the context of this situation or issue would be examined. Chaplains were often encouraged to make brief notes about such conversations so that they could do a follow-up visit in due course. A great many different factors influenced the number of such conversations which a chaplain could have in the course of the day – everything from the quality of relationships he or she had managed to build in that workplace to the pressure of work on employees that day, not to mention the quality of the missioner's listening! As with all Christian ministry, the missioner can only hope that something from that meaningful conversation provokes the person to progress towards a change in their life, or towards taking some action to build greater justice and peace in the lives they touch. At least that conversation may help that person to feel valued and affirmed, their relationship with the chaplain may be strengthened, and they may be more open to change in the future.

Strategic priorities in developing workplace chaplaincies
In attempting to make contact with a great many people largely outside the orbit of the churches, what sort of strategy was employed, with what sort of priorities? Clearly this is a crucial question, because clergy are usually aware that if relationships with particular people in a particular community are established, expectations of continuing contact in the future often arise, and available time is always limited. Regular visiting of workplaces is very time-consuming, particularly if those workplaces are large, and so choices must be made at the planning stage of any piece of Christian mission which will be undertaken by this method. Industrial Mission staff have often been aware that particular workplaces or companies have been (and perhaps remain) major influences on the culture and politics of a town or area, and for that reason should be a priority in making an approach to establish a chaplaincy.

Having said that, however carefully the process of reflection and planning may have been done, the choices about workplace chaplaincies also (inevitably) included a degree of opportunism as well as strategy. Given the dominance of steel manufacturing in the wartime economy of Sheffield, it would have been strange indeed for Wickham to begin workplace ministry in 1944 in any industrial environment other than a steel company. However, the choice of Firth Vickers Stainless as the first steel mill to be approached by Wickham seems to have been led by a previous contact between Bishop Leslie Hunter and Eric Holstrom, the Managing Director of the company, who was personally interested in the Church forming a better relationship with industrial people and issues. Holstrom's enthusiasm for the idea provided a powerful open door which could not be ignored. As we have just seen, Cuthbert Bardsley must have encountered the same open door when he met the employees of Siemens in the air-raid shelters, although he was also impelled by the belief that people who worked in his parish were as much the vicar's concern as those who lived in it. (10)

The type of considerations which led industrial mission staff to make choices of which companies or workplaces to approach to develop a workplace chaplaincy might be these: what is the dominant industry/industries in this conurbation, in the sense of providing the majority of employment? Does this industry have significant historical roots in the development of this city or town? Within this industry, which are the major companies? What insights can the local or regional offices of trade unions offer into the significant areas of employment in the conurbation? Do any of the companies have their headquarters in the city? Are any of the companies significant global players in the world market for their products? Having asked these questions, it would be relevant to ask whether there are any personal links between the churches and senior management in any of these companies which any new industrial mission project might take advantage of to develop the work. Equally, are there any relevant industrial mission contacts with plants of the company in other parts of the country, which could be useful in establishing a new chaplaincy?

It has to be remembered that Britain in the 1940s was still a country in which the economy was dominated by coal-mining, steel-making, and heavy engineering including ship-building. The majority of employment was in all kinds of manufacturing, and in many cities a relatively small number of large companies dominated their communities. It was quite natural, therefore, for the first industrial chaplains often to approach large manufacturing companies – 'heavy industry' as it was often known. Given that in the 1940s, 50s and 60s many people still retained a sense of the church being at the heart of individuals' lives and the life of a whole community – a sense which was slowly eroded over the twentieth century in Britain – these first chaplains were often given access and established workplace chaplaincies. This work flourished and often survived until pressure from foreign competition forced the closure of many of these companies in the 1970s or even 80s. An added pressure was the political decision to dismantle and transfer to private ownership most of the nationalised industries taken by the Conservative government under the leadership of Margaret Thatcher (Prime Minister 1979 – 1990).

Moving beyond large manufacturing units

As large workplaces began to close (11) industrial mission staff became more aware that their portfolio of workplace chaplaincies were not always very representative of the area in which they worked – which was always a key criterion in constructing a visiting strategy. There was also, clearly, a need to find new chaplaincies if IM work was to be sustained. So began the process of diversifying workplace chaplaincy into almost every conceivable employment sector which continues to this day. Differing companies and workplace environments naturally gave rise to differing ethical issues, and in practical terms sometimes required different methods of conducting a chaplaincy.

First of all, a notable example of doing industrial mission work with a network of small businesses emerged with Noel Beattie. (12) Noel began his mission in the local economy when a team vicar in Northampton, when he opened a contact with the local Tesco store, which was situated in the same shopping centre as the church, in 1986. He and a colleague said they were representing the church, that they wanted to understand this new community being formed. 'Can we be around and talk sometimes about what makes this place good or bad for you?' As he says:

Here was an opportunity to reach people in a new town and we were having some results. People were having conversations with the churches because we involved them in meetings which would not have happened otherwise ... We were keeping a rumour of God alive if you like and certainly the church had become a little more relevant for people because of this.

Having begun to experience the opportunities and challenges of industrial mission work, in 1988 Beattie was appointed to Lincoln Industrial Mission, when one of his specific priorities was to develop work with small businesses. As he says of this work (12): 'There was no blue-print for dealing with [the small business sector] anywhere in IM that I could find. So what I simply did was started a small business club because there was none at that time'. He produced a magazine, and brought in people who briefed the members on legal matters and all the needs of businesses. He was very much aware of the personal needs of members: 'there is nothing quite like the loneliness of the small business owner and they become very isolated ... we had some very sad cases where one man in particular committed suicide – his business running into debt and not being able to share this with anyone.' So Beattie was able to offer personal support based on a real understanding of the pressures of running a small business. Whilst visits to such businesses were often not easy he was invited to see what people did at work, and then came the opportunities to talk about the important issues.

In terms of being able to discuss the ethical values of business and connections with Christian faith, Beattie reminds us that many owners of small businesses 'had made enormous commitment, an enormous exercise of faith in actually starting businesses. ... Small business on the whole was motivated by a creative desire to do something from within themselves better than the large businesses they had once been part of. The values were spiritual and included being loyal to customers; going the second mile to retain their goodwill; keeping promises on delivery and cost.' Beattie sums up his experience of mission in the world of small businesses thus: 'Bringing people together was a kind of para-church where they could tell their story and hear the stories of others. Even in the competitive world it was possible to co-operate and respect different approaches and success stories.'

Industrial Mission has certainly not always been confined to companies using traditional technologies. Captain Peter Hayler of the Church Army joined industrial mission work in Cambridge in a dual-role post in 1992 to pioneer work on the Science Park there. He was a graduate chemist with experience in pharmaceutical research, and he attempted to work with the Science Park as a whole. He began by making introductory visits to companies on the Park, and established workplace chaplaincies at three of them, besides visiting the canteens of another two. He was able to be the catalyst and initial host for a meeting of Personnel Officers on the Science Park which continues to this day. He hosted three series of lunchtime talks relating faith to work, and organised two high-tech harvest festivals in local churches, with representation and displays from Science Park companies. (13) It is good to know that this chaplaincy is continuing, and that plans are afoot to appoint a full-time chaplain in Science Parks in Cambridgeshire. (14)

As manufacturing industries declined in Britain, one area of employment which continued to grow and change was the retail sector. One well-known example of retail chaplaincy is at the Metro Centre at Gateshead, the first and one of the largest shopping Malls in Britain, a massive concentration of retail stores in one complex but without the variety of environments to be found in a traditional town centre – without green open spaces, or public buildings like a town hall or museum. This chaplaincy was originally pioneered by John Hammersley, and later developed by the present chaplain, Lyn Jamieson. Besides regular store visiting, she is involved in consultative meetings between retail tenants and Centre management – as is also the case for the chaplain in Telford and elsewhere. She also conducts a regular Sunday service in one of the public spaces for shoppers and any staff that can get away. She supervises theological students who want to learn about mission and ministry in a retail environment, and has recruited and trained some voluntary lay chaplains to assist in this work. New recruits to retail chaplaincy often spend some time training with her. (15)

In 1998 the supermarket company Asda appointed its first official chaplain at its Bexleyheath store, and announced that it wanted to appoint chaplains in all its stores in Britain. The scheme was intended to offer another level of support for staff, but chaplains were also expected to relate to customers. 160 local ministers of different denominations and faiths were indeed appointed in half of Asda's 300 stores, but it is fairly clear that the company expects chaplains to do a pastoral job with staff and customers, rather than to enquire too closely into the moral issues of that company or industry. (16)

Industrial Mission continues to diversify, as the nature of employment in local economies continues to change – and it is worth noting that even in a British society in which religious practice continues to decline, there seems to be a continuing demand in at least some institutions for some kind of chaplaincy or 'faith presence'. A survey the authors carried out amongst those attending the 2008 Industrial Mission Association National Conference at Sterling indicated the largest proportion of chaplaincies (34.5%) were being conducted in local authorities, with 31% in engineering or manufacturing, 27% in retail, and 24% in the emergency services.

Mission and ministry in the context of a local authority clearly requires careful consideration of the political dimensions and ministry to councillors, besides planning how to relate to large numbers of administrative staff in large open-plan offices, as well as industrial staff. One chaplain to a large local authority reports that she has been consulted on equality issues and has been involved in training on spirituality within the social work department. (17) Another is very grateful for the way in which her local authority supports the ministry of 'street pastoring' which she has initiated amongst the clubs in her city centre. (18)

Chaplaincy in the police, fire and rescue and ambulance services is now quite common in different part of Britain. Police chaplains now have their own national body, the National Association of Chaplains to the Police, and to date there are some 400 voluntary chaplains, plus some paid by the police on a full-time or half-time basis. (19) As with all chaplaincy in different fields, there is a proper issue about the degree of independence of police chaplains from the institution to which they minister, and this issue is examined in more detail later in this chapter. All workplace ministry in the emergency services requires much sensitivity to the challenges and pressures which this work demands of those employed within it, willingness to absorb a considerable amount of technical information, and considerable flexibility in order to find suitable opportunities to be able to talk freely to staff and develop relationships with them.

Workplace chaplaincy can also now be found in transport sites and enterprises, and not least in airports. A large airport does seem like a diverse modern community, with a wide variety of employers from government agencies and international airlines to small stores and taxis, and a wide variety of employees from highly-paid airline pilots to poorly-paid cleaners. The issues for a chaplain working in this environment may include having to deal with refugees and asylum-seekers, as well as the stress of some passengers in having to leave loved ones behind, or the stress on staff. Having a person on hand who can both care for individuals and focus the concerns of the whole community can be useful. Workplace ministry also occurs in energy generation, economic regeneration work, the media, sport, banking and finance, call centres, the Courts Service, a few large construction sites, and in some unemployment centres.

Negotiating a new workplace chaplaincy

Industrial Mission would never have become established in post-war Britain unless the managing directors, personnel managers, senior trade unionists and others with whom practitioners negotiated had often had good experience of clergy in the past and usually implicit trust in their work. We have already seen that Cuthbert Bardsley modelled his ministry in Woolwich on a Forces 'padre'. Denis Claringbull (20) witnesses to the fact that when Bardsley went to become Bishop of Croydon around 1950 he approached 30 local industrialists to provide a chaplain to local industry on the same basis as a Forces padre, and so inaugurated Croydon Industrial Mission. Even if senior managers had had no experience of service padres, a considerably larger proportion than now attended church, even if only occasionally, and residual knowledge of the role of clergy was far more widespread in society as a whole than it is now. Whilst these factors cannot be quantified, they undoubtedly meant that (all things being equal) it was considerably easier to negotiate a new workplace chaplaincy in 1960s Britain than it is now.

So how has the actual process of negotiating a new workplace chaplaincy been approached? (21) This task is usually undertaken by a team leader or experienced chaplain, often accompanied by the person who may become the new workplace chaplain (if the process is successful). Let us assume that an interview has been arranged with the managing director and personnel director of a large local company, with the purpose of discussing the possibility of setting up a workplace chaplaincy there. Experience has shown that it is important for the IM practitioner to do the negotiation in person, and avoid letting someone else do it for him or her – the result is usually disastrous! This meeting has also usually achieved best results if the chaplain has met these particular senior managers on a previous occasion, and established some friendly rapport with them. In view of the importance of this meeting – the existence or non-existence of a workplace chaplaincy depends upon it – an experienced chaplain might use a technique such as asking for a conducted visit round the company first, with a brief interview with the managing director. Alternatively, he or she might become a member of a local network such as the Chamber of Commerce, or local branch of the Institute of Personnel and Development, British Institute of Management, and use it to meet senior managers of local companies and discuss issues with them. Establishing friendly professional relations quickly with these two potential senior colleagues in the possible chaplaincy has been found to be important before the subject of chaplaincy gets mentioned.

The industrial chaplain would often begin the discussion by recalling his or her particular responsibility – as a member of the local Industrial Mission team, specifically authorised by the Churches of the area, or perhaps by the local Bishop. Senior managers, as people with authority, need to know that the practitioner is properly authorised for this work, and to whom he or she is accountable – and they respect it. The chaplain might continue that he or she is there to express God's concern for the **whole** of life (including working life), and God's care for everyone, regardless of what they believe, or whether they attend a place of worship. The consequence of this is that if a chaplaincy were established, regular visits to the site would be made (weekly or fortnightly, depending on numbers working on site), and the chaplain would aim to meet everyone employed there within a reasonable time, and thereafter would be available to listen to employees' concerns. If the chaplain has experience of operating a workplace chaplaincy in other local firms or on similar sites, it would usually be helpful to mention it.

In any negotiation about a workplace chaplaincy, details of the confidentiality policy need to be agreed, one that would both protect the confidentiality of individual conversations with the chaplain, whilst recognising the chaplain's responsibility to help build a good human community in that workplace. On occasion, therefore, a chaplain would usually agree to convey to management impressions of shop-floor atmosphere or opinion in a non-attributable way. This is clearly a delicate and sensitive part of the chaplain's task, and one to be exercised with caution and good judgement. Such comments would normally be made on the understanding that the chaplain is **not** in the workplace to remove responsibility for good industrial relations from management or union or staff representatives – to whom it properly belongs – but to encourage and help them to develop the best possible working relationships.

The chaplain would need to meet with staff and trade union representatives apart from management, in order to negotiate their support for this work – and experience has shown that this is where it would be important to stress that it is the local Industrial Mission which has made this approach to the company, **not** vice versa. One key difficulty for chaplains has been in those situations in which a well-meaning, paternalistic management has invited an industrial mission practitioner to set up a workplace chaplaincy, only to run into the suspicion that they have done it in order to spy on their employees!

The chaplain would need to ensure that he or she would have access to employees in all areas of the company 'without unduly interrupting the flow of work'. He or she would aim to develop friendly relationships with many people in the company, and particularly with the Human Relations (HR) department. The chaplain would need a thorough induction to the business, including a conducted tour of each department, and introductions to key staff. He or she would be strongly advised to arrange for a review of the chaplaincy in that workplace, giving sufficient time to develop the work adequately, but before any mistakes have a chance to fester for too long.

From this description of some of the details of typical negotiations, and the challenging workplace situations in the rest of the chapter which a chaplain may have to cope with, it can be readily appreciated that successful workplace chaplains need a very broad range of skills. Many of these skills – theological, economic, practical, pastoral, prophetic and church-related – have been listed in the document *Core Skills for Workplace Chaplains* which was produced by the IMA Training Network in 1999, and is now part of the national Induction Course for Workplace Chaplains. (see Appendix to this Chapter)

Many other elements in negotiation could be mentioned, but experienced chaplains have often found it important to stress that a workplace chaplain works both for the good of all individuals on site, and also for the good of the whole community there. Whereas he or she might spend much time supporting and listening to individuals, there would be occasions when a chaplain needs to be critical of company policy, or of a particular management (or union) decision. Thus the independence of the chaplain from the control of local management or union officials needs to be established at the beginning. Clearly in an initial negotiation this requires considerable tact, and will be greatly helped in the early stages by solid work in building relationships with the key people, and by good pastoral work.

The independence of the workplace chaplain is of critical importance, because it is the basis on which both management and shop floor employees accept him or her. The chaplain comes in the name of Jesus Christ, but not in the name of one pressure group or political party or another (although everyone recognises that the chaplain will have his or her own personal opinions).This is one feature of the job situation of a workplace chaplain which is different to (for example) a chaplain in the armed services (who is ranked as an officer), or a chaplain in a prison or in education or in a hospital (all of whom are employees of the organisation). The whole issue of whether a workplace chaplain should receive any expenses or salary from the organisation in which he or she is working is an important one for all concerned with Christian mission in the economy, because many believe it has a clear bearing on the independence of the chaplain.

This issue is not new in industrial mission, although as church funding and employing bodies have seen their income diminish in the last 15 years, the issue has steadily increased in importance. The Inter-Church Trade and Industry Mission (ITIM) was founded by Lawrie Styles in Australia in 1959 on an ecumenical basis, and rapidly opened workplace chaplaincies. (22) Most of the chaplains were local ministers who worked on a voluntary basis, and the Mission operated by donations from participating companies until 1981, since when a fee has been charged based on the number of hours a chaplain is on site each week. Interestingly enough, Graham Hardwick, then Team Leader of Mission in the World of

Work (MWW) in Coventry, spent a sabbatical in the 1990s studying the ITIM model and subsequently introduced it for MWW in Coventry. He was faced in Coventry with the same situation as in many parts of Britain now, when the main Christian denominations are unable or unwilling to pay for industrial mission appointments. Whilst such commercially-funded work is not easy to negotiate or administer, once the system is in place it does at least permit some workplace chaplaincy to continue.

Other pieces of British industrial mission are beginning to be funded by contributions from the companies concerned. This is normally through a contribution made by the company towards the total costs of the industrial mission team concerned, rather than in the form of salary payments to individual chaplains. In the funding model at Manchester Airport, a number of major companies involved there make substantial contributions to the total cost of the airport chaplains. This whole practice does beg the question: how easily can an individual workplace chaplain challenge a company on a point of principle, when the future of this work is financially dependent on fees or payment made by that company for chaplaincy services? One industrial mission practitioner who claims that this independence can be protected, in spite of financial donations, is David Welbourn. David was Churches' Officer for Industry and Commerce with Surrey and North-east Hampshire Industrial Mission (SNEHIM) 1990 – 2006. In this capacity he was chaplain at the Defence Research complex at Farnborough, much of which became QinetiQ in 2004, and SNEHIM received a very substantial donation from QinetiQ for David's services. David says (23):

[QinetiQ] indicated its desire for me to be a critical friend in, for example, it's encouraging me to produce a no-holds-barred annual report on the state (people-wise) of the organisation. This I did with growing boldness every financial year-end until my retirement … Our 2005 report (which was a particularly challenging one) caused senior management to task the HR department with formulating an Action Plan to tackle the organisational shortcomings we had highlighted.

The question about whether donations should be accepted or fees charged for the services of a workplace chaplain remains unresolved. Whilst Welbourn's witness is an interesting and useful one, at stake for some people is not merely the chaplain's independence, crucial though that is. At stake is the very purpose of industrial mission work. If this purpose is to discover how God is building his Kingdom through the economy and world of work, and to communicate the Gospel in appropriate ways to modern people, should not this be wholly funded by the churches? Of course we may hope that all sorts of benefits may result for those who receive this mission and ministry, but are these not beneficial by-products of this work, rather than its main purpose for which it is marketed to companies? The debate goes on.

Developing a plan for operating a workplace chaplaincy

Assuming the initial negotiation has been successful, regular visits will have been agreed – probably on a weekly or fortnightly basis – and the induction to the whole business arranged, with introductions to key people. But the chaplain is then faced with a complex organisation and a workplace of 500 – 1,000 or more employees. How to understand what is happening in this workplace community – or at least, the significant events? How to minister within it in Christ's name? How to meet all those who would appreciate talking with you, and who you might help? Most chaplains develop their own ideas and methods, and there is of course no one right way, because the task is almost certainly bigger than the capacity of one individual (however talented), and requires more time than can in practice be devoted to it.

Three different models of a visiting strategy may serve as examples:

1. **The Four-Zone Model** (24): this model is based on the assumption that for IM to take place, chaplains and work people need to have serious conversations about industrial and personal issues in which Christian insights can be introduced. These conversations need to be frequent and regular enough for understanding and awareness to be build up over time. This can clearly only take place with a limited number of people, and may be impossible with everyone in the company being visited. So the areas to visit are deliberately limited: (a) to key individuals to provide the information base for visiting, and maintain a high profile for IM; (b) to key departments in the company, a representative sample of different types of workers, with monthly/six-weekly visits for conversations to build up; (c) to

departments to visit occasionally, either to follow up people met in zones (a) and (b), or to do exploratory visits (in the same way as excavating a trench as part of an archaeological 'dig') which may uncover further areas to visit in depth; (d) areas never to visit, either because they are only incidental to the main business of the company, or where the level of noise makes conversation impossible. When a chaplain makes this selection, he or she must always be aware of those who are thereby excluded, and how they may feel.

2. **The Forth Bridge Model** (25): this model begins with an organisation chart of departments and employees on the site, and assumes that it is the chaplain's task to visit all departments, and (as far as reasonably possible) to relate to all employees. The chaplain constructs a rota of departments, each of which can be visited reasonably in a two-hour visit. This can be combined with giving particular priority to key employees, as in 1(a) above, and must be modified to cater for the needs of individuals or particular company events. This model has the advantage of being seen to be available to **all** employees, but the disadvantage of taking a long time (three or four months) to complete all departments and shifts before beginning again.

3. **The Influence Model** (26): this model simply asks four questions of the people in this workplace community:

   (a) Who relates to most people?
   (b) Who is most pressurised?
   (c) Whose decisions affect most people?
   (d) Who is in most pain?

The effectiveness of this model would need to be judged in practice, and the authors are bound to say that they have never seen it operated, although the questions are certainly important in IM terms.

Workplace-based structured activity, including training

Workplace chaplaincy has always consisted of more than visiting factory departments or offices, however important that may be. 'Snap-break' meetings in Sheffield have been described in some detail. (27) Welbourn's annual reports containing a frank assessment of relationships and morale at QinetiQ have already been mentioned in this chapter – reports which clearly generated senior management thinking and action. Hayler inaugurating a Personnel Officers' meeting at Cambridge Science Park – referred to already above – is not the first such initiative: the late Bill Beveridge (28) convened a Training Officers' Group in North London in the 1960s to discuss issues of common interest and share best practice. For IM practitioners meeting the same issues in different local companies, such initiatives seemed a logical and helpful contribution to improving the quality of working life.

In the early days when management education was not well developed companies frequently asked chaplains to make a contribution to training courses for supervisors and managers. In at least one case a trade union asked a chaplain to contribute to their shop steward courses. (29) However, the largest single contribution made by IM staff to company training was probably in the field of apprentice training. Industrial mission developed in the years in which large and reputable British companies regularly took an annual quota of young people (mostly male in the engineering industry) to do a four-year course to become engineering craftsmen or technicians. Such courses consisted in learning basic engineering skills, setting and operating different machines to produce components to a high level of accuracy, and would usually include one or two days each week learning theoretical skills in the local Further Education college.

However, since young people would enter this course at age 16, companies usually took seriously their responsibility for the **general** education of students, and training managers were usually grateful for the involvement of industrial chaplains. In some cases this involvement took place in group training centres to which apprentices came from a number of local companies. Many chaplains developed apprentice courses consisting of a number of sessions, in which important moral issues such as the value of daily work and different types of work, living with questions in a modern society, and the meaning and purpose of life itself were examined and discussed in a series of different interactive exercises. The aim of each session was to help each student to think about the issues and formulate their views, realising the range of different opinions on each topic – and within these opinions would certainly be those which many Christians would hold. Whilst the quality of these discussions inevitably varied, at their best both chaplains and students regarded them as very enjoyable and worthwhile.

Strategy in industrial disputes

Industrial conflict arises for a whole number of reasons: some would argue that it is endemic, given both the commercial pressures on companies, and the previous experiences of so many people. It can result, too, from muscle-flexing on the part of a macho management or a disruptive set of trade union leaders. In Britain in the last 20 years, however, conflict has been more likely to arise after a shrinking in the market for a company's products, leading to redundancies, or perhaps radical changes in technology which can also lead to redundancies and fewer jobs in the future. Whatever the cause, an industrial dispute in a company with a workplace chaplaincy will certainly give the industrial mission practitioner a problem. If he or she has been doing their job well, they will have gained the trust of members of management as well as of the rest of the employees, including the trade union representatives. How can they retain that trust in a situation in which both parties fundamentally disagree on the issue in dispute without siding with one rather than the other?

This is such a difficult area that many might have some sympathy with practitioners who prefer to suspend visiting altogether until the dispute is settled and the strikers back at work. On the other had, a chaplain is hardly going to enhance his or her reputation for empathising with people if he or she pulls out as soon as a really difficult situation arises. Moreover, most practitioners would agree that a workplace chaplain has a specific responsibility to encourage the best possible relationships in that company, and so a period of conflict cannot be ignored. Perhaps two principles can be mentioned at this point. The first is that it would be generally agreed that the workplace chaplain has a responsibility to understand and empathise (as far as possible) with everyone concerned – senior management, those on strike and their leaders, and any employees who may have decided not to join the strike. This means that he or she would need to remain in contact with all the different groups involved in the conflict. If there are strike pickets at the gates of the factory, the chaplain would usually spend time with them, and then if possible get their agreement to go through the picket line to talk to senior management and any employees still at work. Clearly often easier said than done, but still possible…

The second principle is that whilst paying attention to the statements issued by management, and by those on strike, the chaplain would surely be well advised to avoid letting these statements define the dispute, and so getting stuck between two apparently irreconcilable positions. What are the real goals of both the company and the strikers – and therefore what room to manoeuvre does each side have? Clearly whether the chaplain can play a constructive role to bring a just resolution to the dispute crucially depends on the level of trust which each side is prepared to place in him or her. Whilst chaplains are not expected to have any expertise in the technicalities of industrial relations, by knowing the main parties well, and understanding the real issues in the conflict, it could well be that he or she might be able to prepare the ground for the parties themselves to reach agreement with the help of the Advisory, Conciliation and Arbitration Service (ACAS).

It may be helpful to recall that Sheffield Industrial Mission (SIM) managed to stay in touch with both management and strikers in the very divisive national Steel Strike in 1980. IM staff through the Industrial Mission Association's Steel Chaplains' Network expressed their concern about the proposed closure of the Corby and Shotton plants to Bob Scholey, the British Steel Corporation's (BSC) Chief Executive. The churches of South Yorkshire were kept fully informed and were praying for a just outcome. In the event, after 12 weeks the strike ended without gaining any change in BSC's redundancy strategy – but both sides were grateful for the work of SIM. (30) The same IM team played a constructive role in bringing to an end two further steel disputes in 1985. (31) On the other hand, the considerable personal cost of getting caught up in the very bitter Miners' Strike of 1984 – 5, with considerable political forces at work under the surface, is witnessed to by Stephen Kendal (32) and Tony Attwood (33). Industrial conflicts can sometimes be very large, very complex and very divisive – even amongst IM practitioners. It is perhaps worth noting that the IMA failed to have a proper debate about the Miners' Strike and to come to any conclusion.

IM and plant closures

One situation where IM teams had no hesitation in leaving their independent role and joining a campaign was when plants were threatened with closure. Here the interests of almost all employees including management and the local community coincided. Chaplains with a foot in both the plant and the community often became fully involved.

The enquiry into the proposed closure of the RN Store Depot at Copenacre has already been mentioned (Chapter 1). The Bishop of Bristol initiated and chaired the two-day enquiry, with the Bristol Social and Industrial Ministry team fully engaged. A senior Government Minister gave evidence, and although the closure went ahead the process was far better managed than was at first proposed. Following the Conservative Government's plan to privatise the British Steel Corporation, many large plants were faced with closure or major reductions in staff. In 1982 the huge plant at Ravenscraig Scotland was one of those threatened. A campaign by the plant Trades Unions, local Councils and a wider Scottish business group was begun. A group of employees marched from Ravenscraig to London, joined by the plant's chaplain John Potter. He used contacts through the IM to assist in the organisation of welcome meetings in the towns they passed through. Ravenscraig escaped the axe at that time, and survived until 1992. A delegation of IM staff from other steel making areas visited Ravenscraig to show their solidarity with those losing their jobs, and to support Potter.

Two years later the Industrial Mission in South Yorkshire (IMSY) team experienced some of the tensions which could be caused by the change from independence to campaigning. BSC proposed the closure of their relatively new plant at Tinsley Park, Sheffield. The plant chaplain was Clifford Auckland, a retired parish priest who had committed himself with great enthusiasm to the chaplaincy, and was well respected. A group of steel industry chaplains met with the Managing Director of the Engineering Steels Group of BSC to hear and question the case for closure. Auckland persuaded his colleagues to produce a short leaflet setting out the case against closure, stressing the knock-on effect on suppliers and other local industries. This was circulated to local companies and mailed to every Chamber of Commerce in Britain. Auckland's participation in the campaign meant that he was better able to support the workers there when the plant eventually closed.

However Peter Lee, the Chair of IMSY Council and Managing Director of another Sheffield steel company was very displeased. The Council debated the matter, some supporting the chaplains' action, others opposed. The team were criticized for making their opinions public, and were instructed not to do so in future without consulting the Council. (34)

Perhaps the most complete overlap between industry and local community was in the coal industry, where isolated pit villages are located near the pithead. When the Heseltine closure programme was announced in1992 the coal industry chaplains were able to use their national network to link together pit communities across the country. Not only did this give support to local campaigns but the network briefed church spokespersons including Bishops in the House of Lords. This complemented the National Union of Mineworkers' more expressly political campaign. The NUM welcomed the churches' involvement, and would often ask for help to provide a church leader to appear on their platforms. The IM office coordinating the network called it their 'Dating Agency'! Participating in these campaigns not only put the chaplains in a good position to support individuals facing unemployment, it also led to publication of materials on redundancy (see Chapter 5) and into involvement in schemes of regeneration.

Given we now live in a society in which religious practice is now fairly rare, it is most unlikely that a workplace chaplain would be asked to offer a prayer at the closure of a workplace. However, this is what Tony Attwood says of his experience as vicar of a Yorkshire colliery town, and later a coalfield chaplain:

Living where I was in Bentley, within sight of the colliery winding gear and the unique sound that it makes ... Bentley was, together with Maltby in the South Yorkshire context, the two collieries which suffered the greatest loss of life in the 20th century ... Maltby in 1923, and Bentley in 1931 and 1978 suffered multiple loss of life, and these disasters were in November and their commemoration followed Remembrance Sunday ... When I finished as Coalfield Chaplain in 1995, a wreath was laid on the top of the shafts of the now-demolished Bentley Colliery, and then we marched to the church for a service of thanksgiving about the work which had been possible. (35)

Notes and references to this chapter

1   Malcolm Torry, *Bridgebuilders: workplace chaplaincy a history,* Canterbury Press (2010).
2   Torry, p 36,
3   Torry, p 59.

4 E R Wickham, *Church and People in an Industrial Society*, p 245.

5 E R Wickham, *Encounter with Modern Society*, Lutterworth (1964) p 19.

6 See Chapter 2.

7 See Chapter 2.

8 Sometime Senior Chaplain, Greater Manchester Industrial Mission. The story was told in an email to Mike West in October 2009.

9 M Halsey's article 'Crossing Boundaries' in *Life Cycles*, edited by Elaine Graham and Margaret Halsey, SPCK (1993) p 155.

10 Torry, p 36.

11 The issues involved in ministry at the closure of a workplace are dealt with at the end of this chapter.

12 The information and quotations which follow are taken from an interview with Canon Noel Beattie conducted by Peter Cope on 6 July 2006, and to be found at http://www.industrialmissionhistory.org.uk

13 This information in an email to Peter Cope in July 2010. After a spell with Newport and Gwent IM, Hayler returned to Cambridge as Associate Vicar of Great St Mary's and Chaplain to University staff.

14 In an email to Peter Cope from Canon Chris Savage, Team Leader of Chaplaincy to People at Work in Cambridgeshire (CPW). In January 2010 CPW launched a Science Parks Chaplaincy Advisory Group, with the aim of planning and inaugurating a full-time chaplaincy in this area of the local economy.

15 This information about Canon Lyn Jamieson from Northumbrian Industrial Mission Annual Reports 1997, 1998 and 2000/1.

16 Information supplied by Bob Davies, retail chaplain in Ashton-under-Lyne, from an article in *The Guardian*, 31 December 2005.

17 Article by Cate Adams about her work in Aberdeen in *IMAgenda*, September/October 2008 pp 8-9.

18 Article about the work of Alison Finch in Colchester in *IMAgenda* September/October 2008 p 12.

19 Information supplied in an email by Francis Pole, first National Co-ordinator of the National Association of Chaplains to the Police.

20 Interview with Denis Claringbull (later Senior Chaplain, Churches Industrial Group, Birmingham) conducted by Peter Cope on 27 July 2006 and to be found at http://www.industrialmissionhistory.org.uk

21 Some of the points from this section are taken from *Negotiating Entry to a Company*, a brief paper by Mike West and used on the IMA National Induction Course. A good guide to the theological and practical issues involved in workplace chaplaincy was *Starting the Work – a basic manual for Industrial Chaplains*, Recommended Paper Five published by the Churches Consortium on Industrial Mission (CCIM) in 1982.

22 This information from *Inside Industry – the history of ITIM in South Australia*, Jim Baxter, ITIM (1985).

23 In an interview with Peter Cope on 28 May 2008, to be found at http://www.industrialmissionhistory.org.uk

24 This model originates with Mike West, and has been regularly presented on the National IM Induction Course.

25 This model was the one advocated by Roger Howes, sometime Director of Worcestershire Industrial Mission (who had a 13-week cycle at his chaplaincy at Garringtons Ltd, Bromsgrove), and often used by Peter Cope. It was known as the 'Forth Bridge model' because just like the crews who painted this famous structure, you began at one end and worked your way to the other, and then began again.

26 This model was devised by Mike Lamb and Mike Fox, students on the National IM Induction Course in 2005.

27 See especially Chapter 2 above.

28 Sometime Team Leader, London Industrial Chaplaincy (moved from that appointment 1969).

29 Julian Eagle made a contribution on courses run by the Transport & General Workers' Union and the General, Municipal and Boilermakers' Union. See his interview with Peter Cope in May 2008 at http://www.industrialmissionhistory.org.uk

30 Reported in Paul Bagshaw, *The Church beyond the Church,* Industrial Mission in South Yorkshire (1994) pp 90-92.

31 See Bagshaw, pp 103-4.

32 In an interview with Peter Cope in July 2006, to be found at http://www.industrialmissionhistory.org.uk Stephen Kendal was Chaplain to the North-East Coalfield 1978 – 90, and

Team Leader of Worcestershire Industrial Mission 1990 – 2000.

33 In an interview with Peter Cope in December 2006, to be found at http://www.industrialmissionhistory.org.uk Tony Attwood was Team Vicar of Maltby and part-time Industrial Chaplain 1981 – 1986, and Coalfield Chaplain with Industrial Mission in South Yorkshire 1986 – 1995.

34 Bagshaw, p 103.

35 In the same interview as Note (33).

Appendix

Core Skills for Workplace Chaplains
This is the final version produced in 1999 by the IMA Training Network. It follows a pattern widely used in Industrial Training, showing how IM was able to learn from its ministry.

Theological
This involves showing that I understand why I undertake workplace visiting. I can do this by:
a) Describing, in explicitly theological terms, why I undertake workplace visiting with particular reference to the theology of mission and evangelism;
b) Explaining, in terms understandable to every church why I undertake workplace visiting;
c) Explaining what I am doing there to people of all faiths and none in the workplace.

Economic
This involves showing that I can discover and understand the secular significance of workplaces I visit. I can do this by:
a) Describing what information about a workplace is significant, and how it may be discovered;
b) Describing how the workplaces I visit are affected by forces in the local. national and global economies;
c) Describing the effect of these workplaces on community and environment;
d) Describing the organisational structures and power relationships that operate in the workplaces I visit.

Practical
This involves showing that I can visit workplaces purposefully, systematically, sympathetically, and with confidence. I can do this by:
a) Describing the aims of workplace visiting;
b) Describing how to analyse a workplace and plan a visiting strategy;

c) Keeping appropriate records of visits undertaken and information obtained;
d) Describing the obligations of being a privileged visitor, including health and safety, and confidentiality, issues.

Pastoral

This involves showing that I can relate effectively to the individuals I meet during my visits. I can do this by:
a) Describing how to initiate conversations in the workplace;
b) Exploring connections between people's world views, personal experience and the Christian faith;
c) Developing the skills of listening, and responding appropriately to people's questions, needs, and confidences;
d) Valuing people of other faiths.

Prophetic

This involves showing that I can assess situations at the workplace in the light of the Christian gospel and respond appropriately. I can do this by:
a) Describing the style and ethos of prophetic ministry by a workplace chaplain at the place visited;
b) Analysing a situation in terms of justice and the integrity of creation;
c) Describing a range of possible actions to respond to this analysis.

Church Related

This involves showing that I understand how my workplace visiting relates to the wider work of industrial mission and the local church(es) in my area. I can do this by:
a) Encouraging and resourcing local churches to develop worship which embraces the working lives of the wider community;
b) Encouraging local churches and their members to play their part in mission to the world of work;
c) Describing the ecumenical nature of workplace visiting;
d) Relating my work to a local strategy of industrial mission;
e) Relating appropriately to other workplace chaplains in my area (or, if none exists, appreciating the value of seeking support and further personal development elsewhere);
f) Relating my insights of industrial mission to the wider mission of the Church.

CHAPTER FIVE

Mission Beyond the Workplace

Singer:
But you can hear me singing
to the people who don't listen
to the things that I am saying
praying someone's going to hear,
and I guess I'll die explaining
how the things that they complain about
are the things they could be changing
hoping someone's going to care
'cause I don't believe that
no-one wants to know.

From an old Filipino folk song *The Devil and the Singer*
quoted by Julian Eagle in
A Smouldering Land: Lessons from the Philippines

This chapter more than any other demonstrates the difference between industrial mission and workplace chaplaincy. The latter, which has become a popular term for the work of industrial chaplains, is quite clear: it is work in and with specific workplaces. Chapter 4 has described and explained the variety of styles and methods of workplace chaplaincy, which for most chaplains remained the core of their activity. But from the beginning most chaplains also saw their work in those workplaces as part of a mission into and for the whole of industrial society. Industrial mission points to the links between individual workplaces through economics, politics and culture. Because, they argued, industrial and economic life shapes our whole industrial society, it was an essential sphere for the mission of the whole church.

From this perspective industrial mission always sought opportunities to move out from workplaces in two directions — back to the other parts of the church to help educate them see their role in mission —

and outwards into the economic infrastructure, to employers associations, trades unions, chambers of commerce and government agencies. This chapter first reports on some ways in which IM teams developed activities to work beyond individual workplaces.

Sometimes these activities were directly linked to workplaces in which there was chaplaincy but often into other areas completely. We begin with the story of the Homeworkers' Project of Leeds Industrial Mission. This meets a criticism of most workplace chaplaincy that it is not in those workplaces where employees suffer serious exploitation; such employers do not allow chaplains access. This project shows that it was possible to engage effectively with vulnerable workers. Then we deal with ways in which chaplains developed networks to access key people at national and European levels, responding to the ways that local businesses became branches of national and even global enterprises.

Homeworking – mission with marginal workers
In 1994 the European Union's Employment and Social Affairs Directorate (DG5) held a series of Hearings into the employment conditions of people who worked from home, variously described as 'outworkers' or 'homeworkers'. Two Yorkshire women homeworkers and Dian Leppington, a member of Leeds Industrial Mission, spoke of their experiences. They also reported on the work to organise and support women homeworkers in their area. This built on the Mission's collaboration with the West Yorkshire Low Pay Unit, and the European IM network around the issue through the ECG.

Leppington joined the Leeds IM (LIM) team in 1985. As there was no money in the IM budget for her post she negotiated for a full stipend for five years with the Girls' Friendly Society (GFS) who had provided her house in her previous parochial appointment. GFS's concern was for women at work and Leppington already had a special interest in women's experience of low pay. She exercised a traditional pastoral model workplace chaplaincy at Leeds Industrial Co-operative Society for four years. She then asked herself 'who are the most vulnerable people/workers in Leeds' and used the answers to redefine her post. (1) In 1987 she began to investigate the conditions of workers whose employment package failed to come up to the levels regarded as normal in most factories and offices. In 1990 she finished her workplace chaplaincy to give all her attention to the Homeworking Project which soon had three paid staff.

Leppington outlined her motivation thus:

> *From the beginning I thought that Christ was crucified because he was dangerous; rejected by both the dominant religious and secular authorities of the day because he sided with the poor. Later I responded to the slogan "God's preferential option for the poor".*

These ideas helped her to redefine her post. She joined the management committee of West Yorkshire Low Pay Unit (WYLPU) when it opened in 1986. The Leeds Trade Union Community Resource and Information Centre (TUCRIC) identified homeworking nationally as a major but hidden form of women's work, always low paid.

LIM committed itself to this area of work and with the Low Pay Unit began to undertake research on the amount of home working in West Yorkshire. A research worker from the WYLPU produced the report *Penny a Bag*. (2)

In 1988 LIM, West Yorkshire Low Pay Unit and TUCRIC convened a West Yorkshire-wide Conference, paid for by the Equal Opportunities Commission, which brought together homeworkers, local health, social and community workers, doctors and others. They learned from the Leicester Outworkers Unit which was supporting outworkers in that city. LIM gained a grant from the Church Urban Fund (CUF) to employ two outreach workers, both Sikhs. They produced a Homeworkers Information Pack (based on the Leicester Outworkers Pack). They took a stall in Leeds open air market handing out leaflets and copies of the pack. Regular meetings were begun for local homeworkers in a community centre in Mixenden Halifax, using its child care facilities and supported by the Centre's Community Worker. Later the West Yorkshire Low Pay Unit obtained European Union funds and money from Oxfam, making it possible to employ three full-time staff, all ex-homeworkers.

Through the European Contact Group for Urban and Industrial Mission (ECG) contacts were made with other teams across Europe working on women's employment issues including homeworking. In

1988 Leppington and the two outreach workers attended an ECG Consultation in Paris on *Migrant women across Europe*. Later that year three Yorkshire homeworkers attended an ECG training workshop in Italy. A key element of their European collaboration was the campaign to have homeworkers treated as 'employees' rather than 'self employed'. This eventually led to the International Labour Organisation referring to 'workers' rather than 'employees' in their recommendations on employment rights. In Britain local authorities began to extend their Health and Safety activities to include homeworkers, with rules for sound proofing, smoke detection and other hazard information, which gave the project some new tools for challenging the providers of home work.

Using the ECG network exchange visits were made to homeworking projects in Portugal and the Netherlands (1990), France and Italy. In all these activities, whether under the banner of LIM, the Low Pay Unit or TUCRIC, Leppington played a leading role. In addition to her organising skills she also brought an awareness of the importance of the personal dimension to all meetings, often around shared food. In this way the confidence of these poorly paid women participants was increased, and they retained control of these events.

These achievements were only possible with the time and resources of a full-time IM post, as well as Leppington's commitment and personality. It fully demonstrated that with appropriate resources IM could effectively tackle issues of poverty and injustice, but not at the same time as preserving its uncommitted stance in workplace chaplaincy.

Leppington left the LIM team in autumn 1997 to become Chaplain at the University of Teesside. Funding from both the churches and grant-making bodies became harder to acquire at that time, and LIM's direct involvement with the project came to an end in 2000.

National Industrial Mission – networking across Britain
Wickham had provided a theoretical model for the need for expressions of the church's mission at city and national level. In Sheffield he established the Mission at city level. The Report *The Task of the Church in Relation to Industry*, whose Secretary was Wickham, argued for a need for industrial mission work at national level to be undertaken by specialist national officers of the church. (3) That proposal came to nothing, but IM teams were able to create

networks that attempted the national task – they called it 'National Industrial Mission'.

In *Church and People in an Industrial City* Wickham has this diagram. (4) It illustrates 'the social projections and power points of functional structures of society falling outside the impact of the territorial structure of the church (i.e. parishes)'.

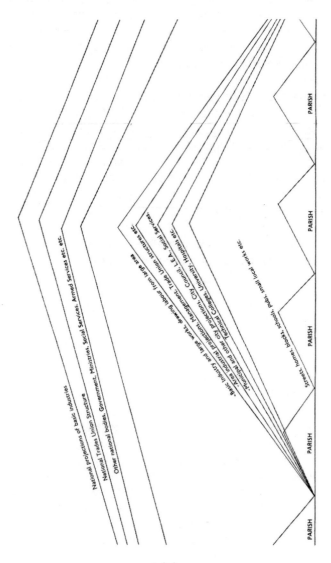

The history of IM teams' collaboration at a national level has been outlined in Chapter 1. What were the objectives of these programmes and how did they come about? In answering the question 'what are you doing here?' chaplains usually began with 'trying to understand what is going on'. This involved getting the broadest possible picture of the company visited, necessarily involving the national (and even international) context. The very large plants visited in the early days were almost all part of national companies. Senior plant management already had a national perspective. In most cases there were also national trades union combines. Reading company documents and newspaper articles was no substitute for personal experience. Long before the title National Industrial Mission was coined in the late 1970s teams had developed contacts with each other. When new chaplains were appointed a favoured part of their induction training was to visit the larger established teams particularly Sheffield, South London and Manchester. One reason for selecting teams to visit would be that they worked in the same industry or even the same company. Sheffield in particular played a significant role in this induction training, including long-term placements. (5)

Networks in national industries – steel, rail etc.

These personal contacts led to an annual meeting at which chaplains in the steel industry shared their experiences. In the early decades IM was at its most concentrated in the steel industry: steel plants everywhere were dominant features in their local economy and its workers typically estranged from the churches. Almost every major steel works in Britain had a chaplain in the 1970s. As managers were promoted from plant to plant chaplains passed their names to each other and contact was maintained. This extended to the management headquarters in London. Chaplains invited senior managers to their annual gathering, and when that took place in London they visited the people in the British Steel Corporation head office whom they had known at plant level. A similar process took place with the major trades unions in the industry. From the mid-1980s the Iron and Steel Confederation, representing process workers, invited two chaplains to attend their annual residential conference as the union's guests. Chaplains organised a rota so that each member attended for two consecutive years.

Chaplains in other nationwide major employers soon developed their networks. The 13 chaplains working in different parts of British

Rail formed their network in 1971 and by 1978 were meeting regularly with BR directors and national officers of the railway unions. The networks in the Central Electricity Generation Board, the Fire and Police Services all held their annual meetings in conference centres owned by the employers, often at the employer's expense. It is notable that all these examples are in nationalised industries, and it may be that the culture in these at those times was more open to the chaplains' work. Networks in the car and aerospace industries also existed but did not develop similar relationships with national level management. The fact that many chaplains were in full-time posts made it possible to for them to find time for these meetings, and in the 1970s and 80s there were sufficient funds in IM teams to meet the travel costs. From 1980 the IMA allocated some of its funds to support the creation of new national networks, and assist some of their activities.

These meetings enabled chaplains to share best practice in similar situations and to develop their understanding of the company and industry as a whole. Both immediately fed back into their work 'at home'. It enabled chaplains to demonstrate their serious concern for the company. Where these meetings involved national management or national trades union officers there was the same assumption of confidentiality on which all industrial information was shared. If there was an element of negotiation it was about improved facilities and access for chaplains at plant level.

Networks around common concerns

These examples of National Industrial Mission grew out of the chaplains' presence in plants across the company. A different version of National Industrial Mission was rooted in IM teams' concerns for issues at local level, especially where that led to project work and contact with government agencies. As unemployment grew in the 1970s many teams became involved with Government schemes for unemployed people, chaplains often serving on management committees. In some they contributed to the Life and Social Skills training sessions, using materials developed for use with apprentice groups in companies. It was natural for them to seek meetings with civil servants directing the schemes at regional and national level. There were regular meetings with the Chairman and senior staff of the Manpower Services Commission. As these meetings concerned Government policy, about which there was

Richard

open and public discussion, chaplains hoped that their direct experience of the schemes at local level might affect policy-making. For example, teams generally agreed that the funding for schemes was insufficient to provide good training and placements. (see Chapter 1) But this was wishful thinking. One chaplain commented, 'They listen to us politely but it is as if some lower level civil servants were reporting; there would be no change of policy!'

Both models of National IM gave chaplains a better understanding of the forces and personalities at work, and thus enabled them to enter more fully into dialogue at local level. It also demonstrated their commitment to the industries and communities they served; as a result senior managers and trades union officials took IM more seriously.

Networking at the European level

The sense of common understanding and purpose which helped IM staff in Britain to collaborate in building networks and links within national companies or around shared interests was also true on an international scale. Within Europe this was carried forward by the creation in the late 1960s of the European Contact Group for Church and Industry (later ECG for Urban Industrial Mission). It was recognised by the World Council of Churches Urban Industrial Department as its regional partner for Europe. The funding for its Annual Meeting came from national church bodies and in Britain from the IMA. In the 80s the WCC made available some funds to support international projects. The major participants, in addition to Britain, were West Germany, the Netherlands, Switzerland and protestant groups in France and Italy. There were also participants from East Germany, Hungary and Czechoslovakia though in some years the East-West tension was such that they could not attend the Annual Meeting. Participants were nominated by IM teams or national church bodies, and usually served for three or four years, creating a network of people who had good contacts in the other countries. As the working language of the ECG was English members were glad to have one of the two British members serve on the Executive, as Chairman, Secretary or Treasurer.

Contacts at and through the ECG enabled many teams to develop links to IM groups with similar interests in other countries. In the other countries few teams had British style in-plant contacts and most exchanges focussed on general industrial and employment issues. In 1974 the *IMA Newsletter* noted that there were ten active exchanges between British teams and teams elsewhere in Europe; a year later there eighteen. Most were in Germany or France with one to Poland in 1981. (6) Some were short lived, others continued for over twenty years. Rather than sketching a large number here we record in some detail two very different projects. One, built on connections between different parts of the same employer, focussed on developing workers' and their trades unions' understanding of their global employer, and the other focussed on the issue of vocational development in two, and later three, countries. The common features are the trust between IM staff in different countries, the personal scale of the activities, and the organisational and language skills of the staff engaged.

Meeting the challenge of the Multinationals
On Monday August 6th 1973 the train bearing the party of Vauxhall shop stewards drew into Mainz Railway station. A sudden thought struck Mike West. He had been the Industrial Chaplain to Vauxhall Motors Luton for three years, building on the work of the first-full time chaplain in the town. He had a good relationship with the powerful trades unions in the company, but taking this party to Germany would test that to its limits. The week's programme including organising host families and making contact with the Opel trades unions was wholly in the hands of the Industriepfarrer (Industrial Chaplain, but with a different role to industrial chaplains in Britain) Max Gutknecht-Stohr. But West had never met him, only spoken a few times on the phone: could he be trusted to deliver or would the whole enterprise set back West's work with the Vauxhall trades unions for years?

A year before in August 1972 Peter Duncan, Industrial Chaplain in the London Docks had phoned West one Sunday lunch time. He explained that he had a party of Hamburg dock workers visiting. It was led by the IM worker there, who was about to move to the IM team in Russelsheim, the headquarters and main factory of Opel Motors, and who would like to speak to West. In the brief conversation which followed the two established their common interest in the two General Motors (GM) companies in Europe, which at that time were beginning to integrate their design and manufacturing operations. Would West like to organise a visit by Vauxhall trades unionists?

West responded positively and began to talk to trades union leaders in Luton. There was much talk of the ways that Luton management compared their productivity unfavourably with the Germans, and who used that to demand higher output. Later they learned that Opel management used to threaten to move work to Vauxhall where pay rates were lower than in Germany! The ECG had been studying what were then termed Multinationals (MNC), and at their 1976 Annual Meeting had asked IM teams across Europe to use their contacts to assist workers, who felt threatened by their multinational employer, to meet across country frontiers. (7)

Here, on the basis of common interest and an assumed trust, the two IM teams had created a fragile bridge across which GM workers could cross, meet and perhaps in time collaborate. This first visit was a group of volunteers taking a week of their annual holiday. Some were funded by their TU branch; others came at their own expense. The visit was an unqualified success: visits were made to the Opel works, a smaller engineering firm, a trades union residential college, and a secondary school. The Mayor of Russelsheim, an Opel worker, hosted a lunch. Every part of the programme was carried forward with Gutknecht's enormous energy, and his faultless translations. But for the more committed members it was the meetings with Opel trades unionists which had the greatest effect. At a meeting of the Russelsheim Trades Council, dominated by Opel trades unionists, West summed up the unanimous agreement in his creaky German 'the question is not shall we meet again, rather when shall we meet again'.

On their return to Luton the group prepared a detailed report on their findings. It included not only the rates of pay but also an estimate of the cost of living in Germany. This showed that although pay rates were significantly higher they did not result in a higher standard of living. The dates of the return visit were quickly fixed, and a programme developed. Housing the visitors with local families which had been a valued feature in Russelheim was repeated on this and most exchanges until the mid-1980s. Finding hosts amongst Vauxhall workers was not difficult. Works visits and several meetings with trades union groups quickly filled the programme. Vauxhall management were less than enthusiastic but could not refuse works tours and at least one free lunch.

On 16th September 1974 the first German party arrived, composed of ten Opel workers, seven from Russelsheim and three from the Opel plant in Bochum, plus all four members of the Russelsheim IM team. It was easier for the Germans to obtain funding: those who were members of the Workers' Council (Betriebsrat – established under the German Co-determination Law) claimed from their education fund, although visits to other GM companies could not be regarded as Workers' Council business. Others were part subsidised by trades union funds or paid for themselves. The divided responsibilities of the Metal Workers' trade unions and the Opel Workers' Council made it harder for the Germans to adopt the exchange programme as official business. Thus whilst the Vauxhall unions made the programme official in 1976, in Germany it continued to be an IM project. West participated as convenor/facilitator of the Luton end of the programme until his appointment ended in 1981.

The ECG had allocated some funds to its MNC project and with that West was able to fund the travel costs for four senior Vauxhall trades unionists (and himself) to visit Germany in December 1975. Their seniority meant that the visit could take place in works time without loss of pay, and opened doors to the leadership of the Workers' Council in Russelsheim. The success of this visit led to the adoption of the programme by the Vauxhall Joint Trades Union Committee.

The next pair of visits were delayed by industrial relations problems in both countries. The eleven who visited Russelsheim in February 1977 included for the first time representatives from the Ellesmere Port plant, and the German visit to Britain 13th – 20th April 1980 included 36 hours in Ellesmere Port.

In the 1980s trades unions recognised that transnational cooperation was essential and contact was taken up by regional and TU national officials. Later European regulations created a process for forming European Workers' Councils and by the end of the 1980s there was a General Motors Europe Trades Union Council. John Peart, West's successor in Luton, was not as committed to the trades union movement and the project ceased to be linked to IM. Max Gutknecht continued to be involved for longer, not least because of his contribution as an interpreter, but there too it ceased to be an IM project.

IM in the two countries had played an important part in breaking down the suspicion between two groups of workers within the same

MNC; they found much that united them at personal and political levels in the face of their powerful employer. A basis for cooperation had been established making it harder for General Motors to play them off against each other. More importantly, personal experience and personal contact had been added to the trades union slogan of international solidarity. In other places church bodies had studied and reported on transnational corporations; the IM teams in Luton and Russelsheim had brought that to life.

Studying vocational development in three countries (8)

Trevor Cooper entered Das Haus des Lehrers, the Berlin Headquarters of the German Democratic Republic's (DDR) State Education System. At the Reception desk he introduced himself in rusty German:

Good day. I am from Coventry, England, an Industrial Chaplain based at the Cathedral. With my colleagues in West Berlin we conduct educational exchange visits for young workers. It would be good if we could include in our programmes the opportunity to learn more about the system of education and training here in the German Democratic Republic. I wonder if I might see someone to discuss the possibilities?

With the assistance of a teacher from West Germany who was waiting in the reception area, Cooper met a senior official who provided names of suitable contacts and expressed the hope that such visits could go ahead.

Coventry IM was based at Coventry Cathedral, which had forged links to the churches in West Berlin since the end of World War Two – a programme focused on reconciliation. By 1969 the contacts made by the industrial chaplains had largely died away until Horst Czock, the team leader of the Kirchliche Dienst in Arbeitswelt (KDA) Youth Department in Berlin, took the initiative. KDA was the national umbrella organisation for the West German protestant church's work with industry.

He visited Coventry with a proposition for an exchange of young workers. All young workers in West Germany were guaranteed paid educational day release and an annual two week residential programme aimed at developing citizenship. The church in Berlin offered many programmes under that provision.

Czock planned to bring groups to Coventry, and wanted a partner to conduct educational exchange programmes in Berlin for visiting groups of young British workers. Cooper, who had only joined the IM team as a full-timer in 1969 volunteered to be the Coventry organiser.

Young worker exchanges were arranged but Cooper moved the focus from young people to professionals responsible for young workers' training and career advice. He assembled a support group with representatives of a wide range of organisations in Coventry: the City Council, the Polytechnic, the College of Technology, British Leyland, Rolls Royce, Dunlop, Massey Ferguson and two major trades unions.

They nominated and paid for a group of twelve who visited Berlin in 1970. Only one had been to Germany before, some had never been abroad and many still had deep prejudices as a result of war experiences. Cooper's careful briefing, Czock's excellent programme of visits and meetings, together with some spare time spent with the host families combined to overcome all their reservations. On their return to Britain the group participated in setting up and carrying through a return visit to Coventry.

This began a series of exchanges which continued for twenty years. The package was varied, depending on the particular interests of the participants and the changing industrial and political situation. Visitors to Coventry were usually accommodated with local families although sometimes the Germans were housed in the British Leyland Management College. The Coventry parties stayed in the West Berlin Young Workers' Hostel run by Evangelische Industriejugend, the youth department of KDA Berlin.

The first visit included a day's excursion as tourists to Berlin East, the capital of the DDR. This led Cooper to propose and then organise exchange visits at first for young workers and later for professionals to Berlin East which included contributions to the programme by various East German organisations. Initially each input was organised by the state-sponsored youth movement the Freie Deutsche Jugend (FDJ). Later programmes included meetings organised through the Gossner Mission, a church affiliated body operating in both East and West Germany, and through the Chaplaincy of the Humboldt University. Visitors were then able to meet young people informally away from the influence of the FDJ.

Both young workers and professionals were able to appraise the relative strengths and weaknesses of the technical education systems and the methods of production employed in the two parts of the divided Germany as well as Britain. Central to this and all other IM exchange programmes was the opportunity to relate at a personal level, in the words of the participants, to 'people like us but in a different context'.

The programmes usually included time spent with families. Sensitively arranged by the chaplains, a wider circle was, therefore, drawn into the experience of the groups. As a result of such weekend hospitality the participants, especially the young workers, grew in confidence and openness in the discussions about industrial, political and social issues.

It should be remembered that the exchanges began only twenty-five years after the end of World War Two and, when they involved the DDR, crossed the boundary between east and west, between capitalism and communism. The professional trainers and managers not only learned how training and management procedures had been shaped by external political and cultural forces, but as they explained their own situations to the German participants they saw those too in a fresh light.

They also experienced the church in a new role, handling secular concepts in such a way as to reveal underlying human and ethical issues. Cooper summarises the result of the exchanges '[they created] fertile ground on which ideas and questions relating to human values, concerning the well being of individuals and the conduct of the social infrastructure could be raised'. (9)

Thirty major British companies, twenty-one local authority bodies, and six trades unions took part in the exchanges, either nominating young workers, or managers or both. Whilst the economic and political climate in the 1970s and 1980s supported such ventures, they became more difficult to organise and finance in the 1990s. They ceased when Cooper left the Coventry IM team in 1992. For the last ten years of his appointment there was growing pressure from the Diocese of Coventry to terminate the post. Cooper submitted his research into the vocational development of young workers based on twenty-five years' experience as industrial chaplain in Coventry, to the Centre for Education and Industry from the University of Warwick which granted him an MA.

The Global Perspective - concern for South Africa.

IM's international involvement went beyond Europe. For a time it was regarded by some churches in Africa and Asia as a potential model for their interaction with industry. Church leaders visited IM teams and experienced chaplains were recruited to new posts: Roy Newell to India and Ivor Clemitson to Singapore. In 1978 Teesside IM had a Japanese minister seconded for a year (10); IM in South Yorkshire a Nigerian priest in 1991. (11) In 1988 Brian Cordingley spent time in El Salvador. (12) This led to a long-term commitment to supporting development in that country, through the formation of a UK-based charity 'Wellsprings' to support community economic development in El Tular, an El Salvadorian village. Cordingley continued this activity into his retirement, regularly visiting El Tular as a trainer/consultant. (13)

All these contacts and experiences fed into IM's general appreciation of the industrial and economic life of the world, but they did not usually feed into specific pieces of work. The exception was IM's active concern for South Africa, sparked in 1973 when reports on the wages and conditions for workers in South African subsidiaries of British companies began to be published. (14) Where chaplains were active in those companies the issue was frequently discussed. Also in that year the Church of England Board for Social Responsibility produced a short paper drafted by Gonville ffrench-Beytagh, *10 questions for employers with South African subsidiaries and 10 questions for their trades unions*. (15) The Church Commissioners began to withdraw their investments in South African companies.

Within the IMA the driving force in raising the issues around the UK links with South Africa was Julian Eagle. He was a full-time chaplain in the Diocese of Winchester based in Southampton from 1965 until his retirement in 1997. Much of his work in the earlier years was in the docks. He was challenged by words of Bishop John Taylor in his enthronement sermon in 1975 about the need to connect the places we are linked to through our work to 'home' – the place to which we belong. Eagle records:

So I began to think about Durban's links to Southampton; the same box of cargo, the same kind of crane but in South Africa the dockers are all migrant workers, and they see their wives once a year for two weeks, and have to travel out of the country to see them – Zimbabwe, Zambia, wherever. (16)

Eagle visited South Africa in 1978, meeting with dockers in Port Elizabeth and Cape Town. Through church contacts he was able to meet with younger black and coloured workers, penetrating far deeper into racist South Africa than most European visitors. He was particularly moved by situation in the squatter camps, where he records buying a coffin for a child who died whilst he was on the site. (17) He returned with a burning commitment to raise the ethical issue of our 'neighbours' in South Africa. He did so with Southampton dockers, within the Transport and General Workers Union (TGWU) at local and regional level, with IMA colleagues and within the Diocese of Winchester. Both the dockers and the churches, in different ways, were hindered in responding to Eagle's challenge by their conservative grass roots. He refers to 'the colonels and ladies in flowered hats' who took against him in the Diocesan Synod. (18) He worked with the TGWU to find ways to include global issues in their training programmes.

The IMA formed a South Africa network of those who were sympathetic. Between 1979 and 1981 they developed ways in which not only the South Africa issue but parallel questions about a company's trade with other oppressive regimes could be raised in workplace conversations. The EEC Code for European Companies operating in South Africa, as well as the ffrench-Beytagh document provided respectable background material for use in those conversations. They also contributed to consultations with the GS BSR and British Council of Churches, who produced position papers on ways of opposing apartheid.

Corporate Social Responsibility
This section is based on the paper *Building a Network* by Crispin White with his permission. (19)

In 1988 those present at the IMA National Conference, in addition to agreeing 'The Way Forward' (see Chapter 1 note 33) also unanimously passed a motion calling on 'the IMA to produce a profile of major industrial companies covering employment practices, company ownership, social responsibility etc'. The issue of the social responsibility of business had been on the IM agenda for many years. Based in the churches in local communities chaplains were well aware of the social effects of large companies, and sought ways to engage with senior management about their responsibilities. Many had been influenced by the chapter on the 'Social Responsibility of Big Business' in Fred Catherwood's book *The Christian in Industrial Society* (20) and in *The Just Enterprise* by George Goyder. (21) George Goyder had been the principal speaker at a SLIM lay conference in 1953 which led to a project on Social Responsibility in 1976. (22) Milton Friedman's opposition to the idea only served to encourage IM's commitment. He wrote

> *I have called it [social responsibility of business] a fundamentally subversive doctrine in a free society. There is only one social responsibility of business to use its resources and engage in activities to increase its profit.* (23)

In 1987 the meeting between IMA representatives and the Church Commissioners focussed on the Human Relations policies of companies in which the Commissioners had investments. (24) Other teams came at the issue from their concern about the effects of transnational corporations, stimulated by the ECG and later WCC publications. (25)

At the 1988 Conference Bob Nind of SLIM was asked to carry out the production of the profile. This soon became focussed on Corporate Social Responsibility. He immediately convened a group of IM staff which determined that the process would be 'based on research, would collaborate with other agencies both in Britain and internationally, and would seek for actual change in policy and practice'. This approach, significantly different from the normal IM model, would prove to be very creative. Later that year they brought together representatives of Christian Aid, CAFOD, and national denominational officers concerned for world development and racial justice who agreed with that approach and formed a working group which was to grow into the Ecumenical Committee for Corporate

Responsibility (ECCR) (later the Ecumenical Council for Corporate Responsibility).

Recognising that their combined resources were insufficient to take the next step they secured a £5000 grant to pay a researcher to map all the work on corporate responsibility by churches and other groups. An important ally at this stage was Pension Investment Research Consultants (PIRC) which had been set up to represent the Greater London Council's pension fund's concern for ethical investment. A second ally was the Christian Ethical Investment Group (CEIG) a group of General Synod members monitoring the church's investments. CEIG merged with ECCR in 2008. The core of the group driving this forward were IM staff from the South London and South Hampshire (SHIM) teams. They were able to use their connections to church groups with similar concerns elsewhere in Europe, and with the well established Inter-Faith Centre for Corporate Responsibility (ICCR) of the faith communities in the USA.

The report *Churches, Companies and Share Ownership* was published in January 1990. On the basis of this report the group secured a grant from the Joseph Rowntree Charitable Trust for £25,000 for three years. This enabled ECCR to appoint a co-ordinator. They did so by paying South Hampshire Industrial Mission to second Crispin White three-quarters-time to ECCR for these three years. White had been a key member of the group ever since the 1988 Conference and was already – with SHIM's backing – spending a significant part of his time on ECCR. He retained his quarter-time membership of SHIM to root his ECCR activities in the Portsmouth area.

Christian Aid and CAFOD commissioned ECCR to research ICI, as they had projects in Africa and Asia where ICI had subsidiaries. ECCR's report on ICI as a global company was published in 1994. A popular version *Is the best good enough? A portrait of a TNC* was also produced. (26) Throughout, contacts were maintained with ICI senior managers, which made possible an official visit by White to their South African subsidiary. Using local church contacts he was also able to meet informally trades union leaders from within the company and residents of the areas in which it operated. In this White was incorporating the IM tradition of speaking to both (or all) sides of a situation without becoming compromised.

Another company which was subjected to ECCR scrutiny was Shell Transport and Trading. This was carried out by a working group based in Oxford in which Barbara Hayes, an Oxford IM staff member, played a key role. This group became the first from ECCR to raise questions at a company AGM (Shell 1997).

In 1993 ECCR became recognised as A Body in Association with Churches Together in Britain and Ireland (CTBI), helping to establish their ecumenical credentials. In 1994 ECCR became a company limited by guarantee, enabling it to extend the range of its research and publications more widely.

When the Rowntree grant came to an end in 1994 White returned to SHIM staff, but continued as part-time ECCR Co-ordinator until funds for a replacement were obtained.

ECCR asked the question which had often arisen within IM 'How do we define a good company?' But ECCR then went on to undertake detailed research into company activities, publish their findings and feed them back in ways which the companies could not ignore. They also established 'Bench Marks' (27) by which any company would be measured. IM, with its often unclear objectives and ambiguous relationships with the churches, was able to launch ECCR but not develop its own activities with comparable clarity.

Notes and references to this chapter

1 Taken from an interview with Mike West, 17 July 2008.
2 *Penny a Bag* by Jane Tate published by the Yorkshire and Humberside Low Pay Unit (1990). See also 'Home truths about Homeworking' by Dian Leppington in *A Woman's Place...?* edited by Elizabeth Templeton, St Andrews Press (1993).
3 *The Task of the Church in Relation to Industry* A Report prepared by a Working Party of the Social and Industrial Council. The Church Information Office (1959) C.A.1288, pp 34 – 36 'There should be set up a committee under the Board for Social Responsibility with a competent and experienced secretariat' whose responsibilties were to include 'Contact with national industrial organisations'. It was widely assumed that Ted Wickham wished to become a member of that secretariat, but it was not to be.
4 see Appendix IV of *Church and People in an Industrial Society,* E R Wickham, Lutterworth (1957).

5 see Chapter 1.

6 *IMA Newsletter,* 1975 pp 5 and 11; 1981 p 65.

7 The decision was based on a report *Multinational Companies – a working document,* European Contact Group on Church and Industry (1976). See also the World Council of Churches Assembly resolution:

   'We ask the WCC to aid the member churches to undertake research at local, national and regional levels to enable people to participate in the shaping of a new economic order.' Report on the Nairobi Assembly 1975 Section VI; para 78.

   In 1982 the WCC Commission on the Churches' Participation in Development produced a report *Transnational Corporations: a Challenge for Churches and Christians,* which was largely critical of the activities of TNCs and threw its weight behind opposition movements in the Third World.

   When the Church of England studied the issue they were unable to reach such critical conclusions, but offered 'a symposium reflecting diverging views'! *Transnational Corporations: confronting the issues,* Board for Social Responsibility of the General Synod, Church Information Office (1983).

8 Based on *Who goes there? A challenge to Humanity* by Trevor Cooper, Authorhouse (2009). Also an interview with Cooper by Mike West, 5 April 2008.

9 Cooper, p 105.

10 *IMA Newsletter,* March 1978.

11 *IMA Newsletter,* March 1991.

12 *USA and El Salvador Sketches,* Brian Cordingley, William Temple Foundation Occasional Papers No 18 (1990).

13 For details see www.wellsprings.me.uk

14 *IMA Newsletter,* March 1973.

15 Drafted by Dean ffrench-Beytagh who worked for the Church of England's Board for Social Responsibility for six months in 1973; reported in the *IMA Newsletter,* June 1973.

16 Interview by Peter Cope with Julian Eagle, 29 May 2008.

17 *IMA Newsletter,* August 1978.

18 Interview with Eagle see above.

19 Crispin White, *Building a Network,*
    see www.industrialmissionhistory.org.uk

20 H F Catherwood, *The Christian in Industrial Society*, Tyndale Press (1964). Catherwood was an Anglican evangelical, a civil servant who became Director General of NEDC.

21 George Goyder, *The Just Enterprise,* Andre Deutsch (1987). Goyder was a leading Anglican layman.

22 Torry, p 45.

23 *Multinational Companies – a working document,* ECG (1976); *Transnational Corporations – a Challenge to Christians and Churches,* WCC Commission on Participation in Development, Geneva (1982).

24 An article in *New York Times Magazine,* Milton Friedman 13 September 1970; widely quoted in Britain; based on his book *Capitalism and Business,* University of Chicago (1962).

25 *IMA Newsletter,* September 1987.

26 Alex Kirby, *Is the best good enough? A portrait of a TNC*, Christian Action Journal (1994).

27 The *Bench Marks* document can be viewed at www.eccr.org.uk under Publications.

CHAPTER SIX

Industrial Mission and the Churches

*IM has tried to communicate its experiences in industry
to the church through various occasions and channels.
Nevertheless the church does not seem to feel any need
to hear the experience of IM as any more than information.*
Shigeko Matsumoto, *A Critique of British Industrial Mission.* (1)

This chapter reports on some of those occasions and channels and similarly concludes that it had little lasting effect on church policy and structure. But for every layperson who found IM staff too political or rather irreligious, there were many more who were inspired by IM's efforts at connecting Christian faith and their working world.

There was a persistent myth that individual chaplains and the IM culture were anti-church. There was and is plenty of criticism within IM of the church's lack of contact with the world of employment and of local churches' inability to relate to economic structures which span cities, nations or even the whole globe. Wickham attacked the notion that because the Church of England structure of parishes encompassed 'every blade of grass in England, therefore it needed no structures other than the parishes'. (2) Of course many of those who had chosen to serve in IM rather than in local churches had further criticisms of the church in practice. It has to be remembered that the core culture of IM was formed before the Church of England had Synodical Government or the Alternative Service Book, and before Vatican II. Even the myth that many IM staff were in 'full time' appointments, i.e. without local church responsibility, cannot be taken to imply some distance between them and the week to week life of the churches. Wickham himself always had a congregational base, at first in the Shrewsbury Chapel and from 1959 as a Residentiary Canon of Sheffield Cathedral. As new members of the Sheffield team were appointed they were all attached to local churches. 'They preached, took services, and attended Church Councils and Chapter meetings. They provided cover for holidays and sickness'. (3)

The early members of the SLIM team were invariably parish clergy who visited in their own parishes. Later the Senior Chaplain also functioned as the Vicar of Christ Church Southwark, which acted as SLIM's Headquarters.

Anglican chaplains, whether licensed to a parish church or not, usually became active members of their Deanery Synod, and were often elected to their Diocesan Synod and served on its committees. At least two were elected to General Synod. For Free Church chaplains the relationship was equally close. Methodist chaplains were placed within circuits, and preached regularly according to their circuit plan. The relatively small number of Congregational (later United Reformed Church) and Baptist full-time staff members were always attached to a congregation, and became members of regional and national church bodies.

Chaplains took every opportunity when preaching or speaking at church gatherings to report on their work, to relate it and the experience of lay people in their industrial employment to the gospel. They encouraged churches to include references to industry in Harvest Festival services, or to organise special Industry Services, perhaps at Rogationtide. From 1984 Industrial Mission in South Yorkshire created a systematic plan for this reporting back and lay education. Noting that requests for chaplains to preach came from a relatively small section of all the churches in their area they wrote to key churches in the seven denominations sponsoring their work, offering to preach or address church councils, to help plan industrial services and where possible to run short lay training courses. They collected material for use in services, and a wide range of lay training activities. Whilst the response led to many preaching engagements the offer to lead lay groups was muted.

Lay formation

When chaplains were invited to lead lay groups they would usually begin inductively, asking people to speak about the joys and sorrows of their working life. For some this was a liberating experience; something which they had never been asked to do in a church setting. If the group had agreed to meet for several sessions there was time to explore in depth. Unlike groups in the workplace participants came from a wide variety of employment which required some detailed description and explanation. For groups who had only agreed to a single meeting that method was not appropriate.

There was also the problem that some participants were unwilling to expose themselves to the possibility that others might be critical of their actions or values. To avoid these difficulties teams developed simple case studies, often based on their workplace experience. After a situation was outlined people were asked, and sometimes role played, 'what would you do?' Each team developed materials including case studies, slide shows and lecture notes for use with local church groups. Sheffield IM created a light-hearted programme based on a magazine-style self examination 'So you think you are a good driver/husband/cook' called 'So you think you are a good Christian at work'. Participants chose between four options in ten mini-case studies, which were then scored with low scorers being given penances! This led to an overview of the Christian social teaching on personal responsibility, wages, industrial relations etc. Quite a scramble in a single meeting!

To achieve any depth in meetings the preferred option was always a short series. Teams created or borrowed materials for discussion and teaching. In 1991 the Peterborough IM team were part of a Diocesan initiative 'People and Work Programme'. A full-time Director was funded by a group of church members and groups were organised across the Diocese. A 12-page booklet subtitled 'helping adult Christians discover how God is present in the world of work' was produced and widely circulated. (4) The Norfolk and Waveney IM team went further by designing their programme to be accredited by the Open College Network. (5) It covered vocation, spiritual resources at work, putting faith into practice and included a wide range of biblical material.

No survey of the study materials produced by and used by IM teams would be complete without reference to the two-part document *Tools for Fools* issued by the Industrial Committee of the Church of England, and written by its Secretary, Chris Beales. (6) It included a wide range of materials for use 'to help local churches equip their members more effectively for living consistent Christian lives in a complex world'. It introduced a Participative Bible Study method, sometimes known as *A Secular Reading of the Bible* which became popular in IM.

It was universally true that IM teams' offers to run lay groups outran the local churches' willingness convene them. And where groups were started they seldom lasted very long whatever methods and materials were used. Why? Is it that the churches are just too busy?

Some have suggested that ministers prefer to preserve their authority by staying within the areas of life they know and understand – family and community. (7) But there was also a resistance by lay people, based on their experience that work issues are not usually mentioned in sermons or prayers. Chris Sunderland, a member of the Bristol ISR team reported:

> I spoke to one man the other day who had spent the whole of his working life with a company that made aero engines. He travelled the world sorting out issues to do with their engines. At the time he spoke to me he was putting on his choir robes. He had always been in the choir. I said to him "in all that time coming to church have you ever heard anything of relevance to your work?" "Oh no" he replied "Church is for families". (8)

Carol Wardman, Church in the Economy Officer in Manchester, reported:

> A senior executive when invited to join a "Faith and Work" session told his minister "When I come to church on Sunday I don't want to hear some amateurish attempts at the latest political issues. I want to hear about the great things of God". (9)

Perhaps the gap between church and industry, which chaplains cross in their workplace visiting, is so large in the experience of lay people that a more systematic long term commitment by the local church is needed to bridge it. One example of such long-term commitment is in the Parish of Richmond Surrey and its Vicar, Julian Reindorp. He had been on a placement with Teesside IM in 1965 as an ordinand and was chaplain to the Abbey National head office when a member of the Milton Keynes ecumenical team. As Anglican Team Rector in the Richmond (Surrey) team ministry in the 1990s he wrote of his parish programme linking faith and work. (10) The core was a permanent 'Christians at Work' group which met fortnightly during term time for an hour on Saturday mornings. The group also held an annual half day conference. For those unable or unwilling to commit themselves to the group there were occasional evening meetings at which one or more people spoke about their working life. These activities were brought into Sunday worship on Rogation Sunday, when people placed symbols of their work on or around the altar. On other Sundays workplace issues and problems were included in prayers and sermons. In order to learn at first hand

Reindorp asked to visit members of the congregation at their place of work. None of these activities by themselves is unique to him and Richmond; what is significant is his long-term commitment and the variety of approaches to the issue. It does demonstrate what might be needed to bridge the gap.

The issue of how people can be equipped for discipleship at work was debated in General Synod in July 2008. The process was begun by a debate in the St Albans Diocesan Synod created by the Workplace Ministry in the Hertfordshire and Bedfordshire team, led by the very experienced industrial chaplain Randall Moll. This was passed and sent to General Synod accompanied by a background paper from Synod's Mission and Public Affairs Council (MPA). (11) This stated:

A number of studies have shown that many Christians feel unable to raise the moral issues of their work in the context of their church and that their ministers often feel ill-equipped to help people struggling with ethical matters from the workplace (para 5.6).

The background paper proposed that the MPA should 'examine …the resources available for parishes and their congregations to be better supported in dealing faithfully with the questions and dilemmas which arise in their working lives' (para 5.5).

Some research into the Church of England's engagement with the economic sector was published in *Crucible* in January 2011, accompanied by a paper dealing with a number of study guides, prayer resources and other materials. (12) However the process clearly indicates that whilst the church hierarchy recognises the issue of discipleship at work it is only on the margins of church life and little will be done about it.

In most places IM (often now known as Workplace Chaplaincy) does not currently have the resources to pursue the issue with any effect; it is kept alive in other ways. The most earthed in people's working experience would seem to be the London Institute for Contemporary Christianity's Engaging with Work Project (13) led by Mark Greene. Their vision is:

The UK will be transformed when the Church envisions and equips "ordinary men and women" to make a difference where we are, where we spend most of our time, where we have most of our relationships, where others can see the difference Christ makes in our lives at work, at university, with our neighbours etc.

That is very much nearer the missiology of Hunter and Wickham than what we see in practice in both Workplace Chaplaincy and Fresh Expressions.

Ministerial training

Contributing to the training of future ministers was part of IM work almost from the beginning. In 1949 Bishop Leslie Hunter convened a conference of Bishops and staff of the Church's Advisory Council on Training for Ministry (CACTM) at which Ted Wickham proposed periods of supervised factory work for ordinands. (14) Also in that year Hunter and Wickham toured Anglican theological colleges promoting the idea. They first planned summer conferences for ordinands. This was so successful that when the first was organised in 1950 it was oversubscribed by 100%.

From then on Sheffield hosted two programmes for ministers in training. Summer conferences, later called the Summer School for Students of Theology, were held from 1950 until 2003 when recruitment dried up, with a break between 1966 and 1969. An average of eight students, though in some years up to twenty-three, took part for 10 – 12 days. Recruitment was extended to all mainstream denominations from 1975 including Swedish participants from the Diocese of Vasteras after 1989. At first these aimed at educating students about industrial life. The Summer School report for 1986 noted that: 'the School is well established as one of the few systematic attempts to complement pastoral training offered within the colleges' timetables'. From 1995 Sheffield shifted the focus towards demonstrating the IM model of contextual theology in practice. In 1997 two Anglican colleges credited work done by their students during the course towards their degree studies. However, many colleges and students still expected the course to teach them about IM. Between 1975 and 2003 over 250 took part from 33 colleges from all the mainstream denominations, about half of the students were Anglicans, 15% Methodists with Congregational, Presbyterian and United Reformed Church making up a further 20%. As most students were being trained within their own denominational college the ecumenical mixture added an extra element. A student in 2000 commented, 'I have been challenged to think about social and economic issues and problems. It has been a good opportunity to share with Christians from other backgrounds and traditions.' There was always the hope that some students would be attracted to apply for posts in IM. (15)

The second model embodied Ted Wickham's original proposal. A small number of students would spend up to a year living in Sheffield, working at unskilled jobs in the steel industry and sharing in the life of Sheffield Industrial Mission. Between 1950 and 1966, 200 ordinands took part in this scheme, many of whom later became industrial chaplains. In particular King's College London and Kelham Theological College regularly sent students. When National Service came to an end in 1960 the age of most participants fell from 21 to 18 years and a modified model was run in parallel. In this the second half of the year was spent in full-time theological study, led by Canon Roland Walls. In the 1970s numbers fell, and the placement was reduced to three months. With rising unemployment it became harder to secure unskilled jobs and the scheme stopped in 1980.

Sheffield invested time and energy in working with ordinands and its reputation made national recruitment possible. Many teams offered individually tailored placements for students, mostly from nearby Theological Colleges. SLIM took Cambridge students for two months' vacation work in industry with evening lectures by shop stewards and foremen. (16) Colleges invited IM staff to lecture on IM, and in a few cases chaplains supervised students' academic work arising out of their placement.

In 1973 the IMA completed a survey of all the ministerial training that teams were offering. (17) This survey was taken to a meeting with the Church of England's Advisory Committee on the Church's Ministry (ACCM; the successor to CACTM), whose report *Doing Theology Today* had reviewed ways of teaching theology to ordinands. Following the meeting the IMA commissioned five members to make proposals to the Pastoral Training Committee of ACCM (18), in particular to draft a module which would be an approved component of pastoral training. The group warmly welcomed the report's view that the study of theology should be integrated with practical experience, and that in present society this should include experience of industry. They drew up a draft programme for a module to be spread over one term in the second or third year of training. After a three-day introduction to industry students would spend one day per week visiting an industrial company followed by seminars exploring the theological connections of their experience. Near the end of the term there would be a whole day drawing together what had been learned. The IMA authors stressed that this should be seen as an exercise in Doing Theology, not just an element of the pastoral studies course. They also outlined a Post Ordination Training Module of three separate weeks spread over a year studying the impact of industry on society, including on family and community, and developing strategies for ministering in an industrial context.

Clearly these modules would require the active involvement of IM teams, both to organise visits and meetings as well as to contribute to the seminars. In March 1970 Alan Christmas in Slough reported on a programme for new clergy in the Diocese of Oxford with eight one-day visits to places of employment spread over two years followed by a 24-hour residential conference. During the winter of 1971/2 in the neighbouring Diocese of St Albans, IM in Hertfordshire and Bedfordshire worked with the Management Schools in Hatfield Polytechnic and Luton College of Technology to run two In-Service Training courses of nine days on 'Ministry in an Industrial Society'. (19) In the late 1980s the Scottish IM team collaborated with the University of Sterling to develop a series of one-day and longer In-Service Training Courses for ministers attended by some thirty ministers. (20)

The pre-ordination module was in addition to the standard full-time residential training pattern, but a final section of the IMA paper revisited Wickham's original proposal, and suggested a more radical non-residential pattern in which candidates would combine working alongside existing ministers with 'day release' or 'sandwich courses' off the job. It would be many years before the denominations restructured some or all of their pre-ordination training in this way, but the proposals did emerge as an approved Pastoral Studies Module.

In November 1977 the *IMA Newsletter* reported on a conference of Anglican Theological Colleges on 'Education in Pastoral Ministry' programmes due to begin in 1978. Teams were encouraged to contact local colleges to investigate the possibility of running a unit. One hoped-for outcome would be a greater appreciation of the role of IM within the whole ministry of the church. In 1983 the IMA again surveyed contacts between teams and colleges and published these in a booklet circulated to colleges. (21) This showed a variety of ways of delivering the module, ranging from Sheffield's two-week residential course to weekly factory visits supplemented by lectures. When the Pastoral module was revised and downgraded in 2000 the volume of work fell sharply. By then few teams had the staff resources to provide the supervision required for such training, and these programmes came to an end.

As with lay training programmes at local church level, IM was always working against the grain of the church's overriding focus on parochial life and domestic concerns. Donald Ross's comments on the situation in Scotland can fairly be applied across Britain.

The relationship between IM and the theological colleges in Scotland has largely been dependent on the level of interest and understanding of the Professors of Practical Theology and their staff. In Glasgow with its long industrial history and where IM has been deeply rooted one might have expected regular input into courses for divinity students. This however has not been the case. There were sporadic attempts, occasional lectures, a number of programmes planned but that was all. (22)

There was a minority of students who brought the assumption that mission equals evangelism, or whose theological education to date was inadequate for the demands of 'doing theology' who went away confirmed in their view that IM was not 'really church work'. But where students had chosen to spend time with IM teams in whichever mode, their response was almost always positive. They responded to the immersion in industry, grappled with the inductive theological methods and fiercely debated the IM teams' stances on industrial issues. One participant in the IMSY Summer Course wrote 'it is as if we have been told about Doing Theology in college like describing a bicycle, even shown a photograph of one – here you helped us to ride the bicycle'!

Notes and references to this chapter.
1. Shigeko Matsumoto, *A Critique of British Industrial Mission as a response of the Church in Modern Industrial Society*, in GS BSR Industrial Affairs Committee IC/11/85 (1985) p 22.

2. Paul Bagshaw, *The Church beyond the Church – Sheffield Industrial Mission 1944 -1994*, Industrial Mission in South Yorkshire (1994) p 37.

3. Bagshaw, p 37.

4. Reported in detail in *Called to New Life; the World of Lay Discipleship*, a report prepared by a Working Party of the Board of Education of General Synod (1999) CIO GS (Misc) 546, see also *IMAgenda* August/September 1998.

5. *IMA Newsletter*, September 1995.

6. Chris Beales, *Tools for Fools*, parts 1 and 2; part of the series 'Industrial Mission and the Church in Britain Today' Board for Social Responsibility of General Synod (1987).

7. 'Clergy (not all are Anglicans) still feel threatened about being involved in a ministry in which they are by definition not the experts in the workplace issues of their congregation members; they are "lay" and most clergy sadly cannot cope with being in that "weak" position.' An Industrial Missioner quoted in *Called to New Life*, p 33.

8. *IMAgenda*, June 2000, p 10.

9. *IMAgenda*, August/September 1998, p 6.

10. Julian Reindorp, *Equipping Christians at Work*, Industrial Christian Fellowship (2000) pp 53ff.

11. *Faith and Economic Life*, GS Misc 890B, Archbishops' Council (2008).

12. *Crucible the Christian journal of social ethics*, January 2011.

13. For details of the London Institute for Contemporary Christianity's Engaging with Work Project visit: www.licc.org.uk

14. Bagshaw, pp 17ff.

15. Reports on the Summer Schools from 1975 to 2003 are held in the archives of South Yorkshire Workplace Chaplaincy.

16. Malcolm Torry, *Bridgebuilders*, Canterbury Press (2010) p 45.

17. *IMA Newsletter*, July 1973.

18. The full report of 34pp is in *IMA Newsletter*, May 1975.

19. *IMA Newsletter*, November 1971.

20. Donald M Ross, *God it's Monday*, St Andrews Press (1997) p 99.

21. *IMA Newsletter*, 1984 p 24.

22. Ross, p 98.

CHAPTER SEVEN

The Living Legacy of Industrial Mission

*IM has been from its very beginning an extended
seminar in applied theology...In the process
of clarifying its own mission it has raised issues
about the mission of the whole Church in the world.*

IM - An Appraisal (1988) p 49

The task of Christian mission in society now is arguably at least as challenging as it was in heavy industry in the 1940s and 50s

This book is about mission. It has had little to say about the other tasks of the Church – evangelism and social service. This is because our experience, our work has been in this sphere. But we recognise that all three aspects of the Church's task need to be affirmed but not confused. IM and its experiences point to the enormous missionary task still facing the churches. In 1941 Bishop Leslie Hunter pointed out:

*Christian mission in Britain would do well to remember that it
works amongst people for whom the Gospel is no longer fresh.
A better quality of mission and evangelism is therefore
needed, not just 'a speaking war' but a comprehensive witness
of daily living, prayer and social action.* (1)

In the 1940s it seemed quite obvious to many thoughtful Christians in Britain that the most serious challenge to the future of the Christian faith and the churches in Britain was that the majority of working people – particularly working men – had little or no involvement in the life of the churches. The result of a survey of church attendance in one area of Sheffield in 1941 which gave rise to Leslie Hunter's famous Diocesan Letter on evangelism was clear and was typical of the national picture. England had 'become once again a mission field'. Hunter and Wickham understood this estrangement as a consequence of generations of little or no contact with active Christians (ordained or lay), exacerbated by the tremendous pressures of poverty, large families and inadequate housing. They would also have seen the facts that most working men were at the bottom of the hierarchical system of management in most industries, and that training, health and safety, and industrial relations in most companies was rudimentary, important in terms of their sense of self-worth.

In the third millennium the whole of British society is not so very different with similar challenges to the Christian gospel. Church attendance of any social class is now like that in the working class areas of industrial cities in mid-twentieth century, with women still being more represented than men. The British Social Attitudes Survey claims that 51% of people report that they 'have no religious faith'. (2) But there are major differences. There is no longer an easily identifiable 'working class'. A much smaller percentage of the workforce is manual workers employed in huge factories or mines. Most people describe themselves as 'middle class' and their lives revolve around consumption rather than production. Thus a strategy of reaching a significant proportion of the workforce through large workplaces is no longer possible.

In the 65 years since Industrial Mission first began, the Christian presence in Britain has greatly diminished numerically. Sunday Schools have mostly disappeared, and the general level of knowledge of Christianity in the population as a whole is scanty. Official representatives of the churches find it harder to get their voice and opinion heard in wider society. Like industrial chaplains they may have to wait a long time before their opinion is sought and respected. The truth is that Christianity and the churches are becoming ever more marginal to the lives of the great majority of people in Britain, irrespective of social class. The challenge and the opportunities are clear.

The presence of five million or so Muslims, Sikhs, Hindus, and other world faiths is slowly but clearly changing the culture of many of our cities. There is also an increasingly vocal minority who advocate the virtues of humanism or atheism. By the 1960s many of the workplaces visited by industrial chaplains had growing numbers of migrant workers, some of whom were members of other world faiths. Chaplains tried to treat them with the same respect as everyone else. They found that their ministry was accepted and often welcomed by them. Some chaplains (including us) will testify that they have had conversations about the implications of living with faith more easily with such people in workplaces than with many fairly nominal Christians. This experience should be used to challenge those Christians who have been very cautious about approaching Muslims – or Sikhs, Hindus, Buddhists, etc. – to talk about faith, both because they have some awareness that the history of Christianity has not always been friendly to people of other faiths (to put it mildly), but also because they are afraid of being seen to compromise their faith in Jesus Christ as the unique revelation of God's will and purpose. On the other hand, other Christians recognise the need to forge new partnerships with people of other world faiths in order to tackle significant community issues together, and that government departments – and some local authorities too – increasingly want to deal with representatives of all the religious faiths in a given area in a coherent way. Christian mission therefore needs to be so deeply embedded and identified with the real needs of British society that it can respond to them and change its emphasis as required.

Christian mission needs to express its claims and its purpose in clear, accessible language, for example the CCIM document *Guidelines on the Task, Organisation, Appointments and Continuity of Industrial Mission*, which claims that 'through the process of participation, reflection and evaluation' Industrial Mission 'works for the re-ordering of the relationships, methods and goals of industry and commerce in the light of the Christian hope for justice and community'. Equally, Christian mission should never be afraid to make criticisms of contemporary society – as did the Archbishop's Commission on Christianity and Industrial Problems (1919) – although (as with William Temple's *Christianity and Social Order*) it needs to recognise that such criticisms carry the responsibility of suggesting constructive Christian alternatives. A more recent good example of a church report which both made severe criticisms of government policies in a period of high unemployment and many recommendations of constructive alternatives is the *Faith in the City* Report (1985).

The essential basis will be a Kingdom Theology, of God at work in the world, and the Church's role in it

Industrial Mission has usually described the aim of Christian mission as twofold. Firstly, to alert everyone to the coming Kingdom of God, in order that they will recognise the claims of that Kingdom on their lives, and respond by making their own contribution to it. Secondly, to 'make disciples of all nations' (Matthew 28v19), in which we should see 'nations' standing for all human institutions and structures (including powerful economic ones) which have their proper vocation under God, their particular contribution to human welfare. The vast majority of IM staff have based their work on a Kingdom Theology; some began with this as a motivation for entering the work, others discovered its value as they reflected on their experience. In Chapter 2 we set out the ways in which that theological approach shaped the early work. It included the understanding that the Church is essential in identifying the signs of the Kingdom but not the only means of its growth.

Industrial Mission was premised on the presence and activity of God in people, communities and workplaces quite independently of the Church's proclamation of that activity in and through Jesus Christ. There is a good Biblical basis for this – the Prologue of John's Gospel (John 1vv1-18). The first step in mission has usually been seen as the proclamation of what God has done and is doing in and through Jesus Christ – in both word and deed – and encouraging an appropriate response. But it is worth stressing that this activity of proclamation and service points to the activity of God quite independent of the Church. John expresses this as the eternal creative Word or Logos of God (John 1vv3, 4 and 9). Jesus taught his followers that the advent of God's rule on earth is like the growth of a seed which is very gradual and largely hidden from human observers (Mark 4vv26-29), or like a small amount of yeast which has the capacity to transform a large quantity of flour if it is mixed properly (Luke 13vv20-21).

The work of Christian mission begins with identifying the signs of God's love and justice growing within or transforming people, structures and communities in our world. The signs of God's love and justice will be as diverse as all the situations crying out for God's care, but we should expect them to share some 'Jesus characteristics' – compassion for those excluded from the benefits of society as a whole, a concern that everyone should be valued equally (regardless of ethnic origin, gender or other characteristics) and should have a just share of wealth created, a willingness to accept responsibility for the welfare of others, a willingness to accept impartial moral (or God's) judgement on all human life, and so on. We are not claiming here that this theological approach is unique to Industrial Mission. We do affirm however that Industrial Mission, operating in parts of British society which was and is non-religious in culture and language, has been able to identify examples of Kingdom attitudes and values amongst the communities in which it has worked – and to challenge accepted norms and practices from a Christian standpoint.

Industrial Mission came to see itself operating in the 'gap' between the Kingdom and the world – a gap which exists between Jesus' descriptions of the justice and love of God, and the economic and human dimensions of real situations. Wickham believed that the existing work of the Church had failed to put the claims of the Kingdom clearly before the majority of British people, especially working people. He put the relationship between the world and the Church in these memorable words: 'It [the Church] seeks neither to manipulate nor dominate the world, nor to escape from it, nor merely to reflect a voluntarist religious aspect of it, but to understand it, prophesy within it, interpret it, and stain it.' (3) It has been suggested that the word 'stain' is a metaphor from histology (that branch of biology which is concerned with the minute structure of the tissues of animals and plants), and refers to staining a culture in order to reveal the structure and functions of particular cells. Wickham may well have meant that a key aspect of the Church's mission is to uncover the opportunities for God's Kingdom to break into the secular world and the human consequences of opposing it.

In practice these general claims about the Kingdom are inadequate to engage in dialogue with secular people – they need to be contextualised. In Chapter 3 we reported on the ways that IM practitioners in 1970 – 71 began to produce an Inductive Theology. Later they drew on the work of David Jenkins and Ian Fraser in constructing a theological method which could be used in complex ethical situations. Using this method it is possible to develop greater understanding of all the powers at work, and of the relevant biblical and theological resources which could be applied to a specific situation. There are also other methods described in Chapter 3 – the Theological Grid and the Flying Machine – and there are many others. There is no one infallible method, of course, by which it is possible to work out what the best or most Christian course of action might be in any given situation. The most important step is to do some theological analysis – however one might choose to do it – in which all the important features of the situation are examined from the standpoint of God's justice, love, truth and goodness, so that the best possible Christian judgement may be made about the right resolution of the issues involved.

The need to understand the secular world, to develop a contextual theology and appropriate language; some of the challenges to mission

How can the Christian community discern, and help others to discern, the signs of God's Kingdom transforming our modern world if we have a seriously inadequate understanding of how society is now changing, including demographic, employment and economic changes? This is a task which is urgent and continuing. We have shown how Wickham's strategy in Sheffield and his skill in debating in the workplace was informed by his wide reading in economics and sociology. Far more recently, the global financial and economic crisis of late 2008 onwards caused great anxiety and material hardship to millions through the loss of employment and even perhaps loss of their homes. At the same time this crisis has also provided an opportunity for a critical study of the relationship between government and business which raises important ethical questions about the responsibilities of each to all those involved in them, and the population as a whole. Perhaps this global crisis is a *kairos* moment, from which both government and business might emerge more prudent and more sensitive to the needs of people. These ethical questions urgently need informed Christian comment, and it is good to see that this need has recently been remedied. (4)

In order to engage in mission in the modern world with appropriate short-term and long-term strategies, the churches need to be encouraging and investing in partnerships with good academic centres in which theology can be brought together with economics, sociology and ethics, and climate sciences. Theology has a great deal to learn about the future challenges for humankind from such disciplines, but also much to contribute in terms of the values on which to construct future society. In the 1970s and 80s the Church of England Board for Social Responsibility contributed a great deal to fresh thinking about British society through a series of booklets. (5) The William Temple Foundation at Manchester continues to promote original research to strengthen the churches' theology and practice in engaging with economics, working life and urban communities, and to sponsor valuable contributions to Christian thinking. (6)

In order to communicate the results of these studies and thinking they need to be expressed in an appropriate language. Hunter and Wickham knew that they were in the business of finding a new language to express God's purposes for communities, not least the poorest, and those who have no contact with the churches. They knew that for this bridge-building exercise to succeed, they would need to take seriously the pressures on working people in the 1940s: the critical need to balance income and outgoings carefully every week, and to save for health emergencies, new clothes and shoes (especially for children); the need to show solidarity with fellow workers, and perhaps join the union; the terror of being put out of work, or getting into debt. What does the gospel say about all this, especially when some other people seemed to have a more comfortable life? Doing Theology in context involves all this and much more: what now might be called 'inculturation' – the rethinking and renewing of the faith in every human culture (David Bosch). (7) It is significant that the 'inculturation' or 'contextualisation' of Christian faith is seen as one of the principal advantages of the process of church planting in the influential report *Mission-shaped Church* (8). What is not often realised, however, is that such inculturation often leads to a problem in trying to integrate new believers into existing church structures. Thus the process of successfully inculturating the Christian gospel must lead eventually to new church structures better adapted to the new culture.

In order to reach and communicate with particular groups of people in a particular culture and context, Christians in that culture and context need to affirm all that is valuable about it and so to learn to speak the same language. The relevance of the Christian faith needs to be discovered in that context, rather than assumed in advance, as Philip Bloy comments on the early ICF missioners. (9)

In Chapter 4 we have shown how Industrial Mission practitioners, having been accepted into the workplace and learned its language, would find themselves seriously discussing Christian faith and its implications for all sorts of issues. As the movement slowly spread across Britain, they realised that they needed to strengthen and develop the theological base. The Theology Development Group (TDG) of the Industrial Mission Association was formed in 1975 for this very purpose. In addition to providing materials for practitioners the Group also sought to report back to the churches. In his introduction to the first booklet of the series *Working Papers from Industrial Mission*, entitled *Theology and Politics* (10), John Atherton (then Secretary of the Group) makes it clear that the TDG was formed to communicate the thinking of Industrial Mission to a wider audience, and to prepare for a further advance in mission to industrial society in Britain.

The TDG lasted into the 1990s, and produced a number of important sets of papers in the early 1980s. (11) Its importance for our present purpose is that it demonstrates the potential of bringing together people involved in related mission activities in order to reflect theologically on their work and produce material which can be very helpful for themselves and others involved in similar work. As Atherton says about the formation of the TDG:

> ...there was a growing realisation that the essential theological under girding of industrial mission activity could no longer be left to the luxury of isolated individuals. A theology for movement forward in mission to a complex industrial society had to be a corporate activity.(12)

We are not claiming that such corporate activity as the TDG is unique to Industrial Mission, but we are confident that the TDG is an excellent example of the usefulness of such activity for Christian mission, and the virtue of practitioners Doing Theology in the detailed context of their daily mission activities.

Developing the ministry of lay people through their employment, their role in civil society and the third sector

Industrial Mission never denied the truth of the statement that the church's major involvement in the industrial world was through lay people in their employment. However the growing professionalism of the movement and the lack of any large scale success in developing effective lay involvement and training left the problem unresolved. It remains true that for mission to be effective in British society there must be training for those who will conduct this mission in all the places, communities and institutions of which they are a part or with which they have contact – ordained and lay Christians.

Chapter 6 outlines the story of the experience of Industrial Mission working within the structures of the British churches, and undertaking considerable work in training lay people and ministers through all manner of different projects. We must recognise that there has been a degree of mutual prejudice between some Industrial Mission staff and some parochial clergy, and it is as well to acknowledge this. Some would argue that the very genesis of Industrial Mission lay in a consciousness of the inadequacy of the parochial system to reach a great number of working people, and this has been interpreted – often wrongly – as a major criticism of parochial clergy. On the other hand, great efforts have been made by IM staff and parish clergy in many places in partnership in the face of the huge task of mission. The growth of dual-role posts (such as in the Black Country team) and of part-time volunteer chaplains have greatly helped to defuse the old tensions.

In places where chaplains developed good working relationships with local dioceses, deanery chapters, circuit staffs, and fraternals they were invited to preach about mission at special services (e.g. Harvest Festival or Rogationtide), and to speak at lay group meetings. Although IM teams have produced a great deal of materials to use with lay groups, invitations to use them have been sparse. In Chapter 6 we suggest that the reason may lie in the 'gap' experienced by some lay people between the culture of the local church and their employment in industry and that a more systematic long-term programme of activities is needed to overcome it. We reported on the programme in the parish of Richmond (Surrey) by Julian Reindorp.

Another approach to lay formation and training was undertaken by Peter Cope in Telford in 2000 – 2008. Invitations were sent to a number of committed Christian lay people to attend a breakfast meeting at which one of them volunteered to speak for 10-15 minutes on their job, for example as a computer programmer. Meetings were held once a month for an hour or so, and membership grew to about thirty, although usual attendance was twelve to fifteen. The programme each time included 5-10 minutes for prayer. It was varied by inviting people such as the chief executive of the local authority, the police commander, or the head of economic regeneration to speak about their work within the local community. Over the years the members of the 'Engage Breakfast' developed close relationships with each other, and learnt a great deal about practical Christian discipleship and ministry in different companies and occupations.

Another project which had its genesis in the powerful evangelical wing of the Church of England is the London Institute of Contemporary Christianity (LICC), which seeks 'to equip Christians with the Biblical framework, practical resources and models to engage relevantly with issues in the world today': LICC has specific projects dealing with culture, discipleship, work, and young people. (www.licc.org.uk)

A creative metaphor in Christian understanding of a human group is 'the body', with the adjective 'corporate', derived from 1 Corinthians 12vv12ff. This means that Christians should have something of real worth to contribute to the life of any community, in which working together towards worthwhile common goals, working in a principled way according to good values, and recognizing the diverse responsibilities of each as a vital part of the whole, should all be given their due emphasis.

Modern life is lived out in many communities – employment, leisure, voluntary agencies as well as the local community around the family home. The traditional residential ministry of the churches is used to addressing the physical and social needs of these local communities alongside their spiritual needs, if not as often, their other legitimate moral concerns. However, apart from higher education, hospitals and the military in which there are chaplaincies, there are many communities in which the churches do not have a clear representative presence. This is true for almost every part of the private sector, small and medium sized enterprises and the great bureaucracies of national and local government. There are also the communities of the third sector, voluntary associations of people who come together for a tremendous variety of purposes – engaging in sport, in the arts or music, politics, being advocates for the needs of particular groups and voluntarily providing a service to them.

Christian women or men within those communities or groups could and should see themselves as missionaries in that context, as a deliberate part of their Christian discipleship. It will be an informal work of witness, pastoring and prophetic concern. It is important that this work is properly resourced by the churches, and it needs to be recognised, affirmed and supported by the congregations of which they are a part. However, the number of people in any one congregation who share similar contexts or issues may be very small, and so wider networks, including electronic, need to be set up to overcome the feelings of isolation and inadequacy which can easily arise. This will seldom happen spontaneously and requires, at district, regional and national level, some structures with appropriate staffing, though not necessarily full-time.

The task of the church as public institution, which may appoint representatives to other public institutions, not least government; training and resourcing of ministers and church leaders

Whilst the church's influence on public and private life has declined throughout the twentieth century it still retains a significant place in community life, with local, regional and national bodies, professional staff, and buildings. How can these resources be effectively used to support its divine mission in society? We have already addressed the need to recognise and support the work of lay people in their involvement in employment and voluntary work. Here we turn our attention to the role of ministers and church organisations.

The majority of industrial mission work is focussed on workplaces - and the current popular title for the work 'workplace chaplaincy' emphasises that focus. It is found in airports, retail centres, oil rigs, and in the emergency services. 'Chaplaincy' as a model of ministry is of course also common in hospitals, in military units, in prisons, and in many higher education institutions. There are good strategic reasons for this – these communities can be the centres of power and influence in a secular society, and a presence here means that many people can be met relatively quickly, and it is possible to engage with people who understand and can influence the behaviour of such communities and institutions.

We believe that IM's experience of strategic thinking, networking and theological reflection has much to contribute in this area. From the beginning, doing industrial mission even in a medium-sized town – let alone a large conurbation – has been a large and complex task which therefore required strategic thinking. Key people in the local community, in local authority, management and union structures were addressed before anything worthwhile was possible. Even after the initial successful contacts have been made, it was obvious that the task was huge and the church's resources in terms of the number of chaplains who could be employed disproportionately small. This mismatch of task and resources was always been the case with Industrial Mission. Both size and complexity compelled strategic thinking.

As industrial mission teams grew in different parts of Britain, chaplains began regular visiting on different sites of the same industry. The formation of the Industrial Mission Association in 1970 greatly facilitated contact between them. We have already noted the way in which chaplains visiting the same industry began to form networks for mutual training and development. This grew into joint meetings with senior managers and national trade union officials on important issues and was known as National Industrial Mission. Steel, railways, coal and energy generation were amongst the industries within which this took place. National meetings with senior officials were particularly valuable because they brought together the architects of policy at a national level with chaplains who had detailed knowledge of what effects such policies were having at local level. The same networking process assisted the formation of the Theology Development Group, which has been discussed above.

Structures like the Archbishops' Council should help at least the Church of England to address national issues. On the other hand, the capacity of the British churches to address such issues is much less than it was 40 years ago, and the current ecumenical structures of Churches Together in Britain and Ireland and national bodies in each country (Churches Together in England, etc.) are very under-resourced.

The experience of Industrial Mission consistently points to the value of creating strategic networks which can connect Christians involved in mission in different places with a range of people in different communities and institutions around themes of common interest. At the heart of these themes is very often how to respond constructively to current national initiatives, helping the institutions or communities achieve their purpose whilst also helping individuals within them to flourish. Modern technology can make these connections between people without going to the time and expense of physically meeting together over large distances. Such networks can not only offer information or practical examples but much needed mutual support too. The churches of today could surely benefit from developing networks around particular issues, aided by social networking sites, blogs and emails which were not available 30-40 years ago.

With a theology which understood and expected God to have agents, if unconscious, who were forwarding His purposes, IM often collaborated with people quite outside church structures. They worked on projects which aimed to transform the lives of individuals and communities in need with God's love and justice, some of which are reported in Chapter 5. Industrial Mission's experience of working on practical projects with 'fellow travellers' or 'people of goodwill' – people whose own faith is at best undefined – both made such projects possible and strengthened that theological approach. The presence of Muslims, Hindus and those of other world faiths in British cities who share a desire to transform relationships and environments can facilitate enriching partnerships. Thus Christians in today's society do well to look for opportunities of collaboration with all manner of people, both to tap into local skills and wisdom, and also because this provides opportunities for giving functional, practical help where it is most needed. Furthermore, the relationships within such joint enterprises often create opportunities for sharing personal faith more effectively than in other social relations.

When the local churches see their vocation to work in the local economy, they will need to make allies in the local commercial and industrial structures – the Secretary of the Trades Union Council, the Director of the Chamber of Commerce, the manager of the local Economic Development Unit, etc. - but also sometimes to follow the links through to regional, national or occasionally even international levels. Two different models of the churches engaging collectively with the local economy and looking for partners are discussed and evaluated in *Church, Change and the Economy*. (13) One model is provided by the Churches' Regional Commission in the North-East, which gives the churches a valuable voice at regional level, but requires long-term commitment by the churches which may not always exist. Another model is the Council for Social Responsibility (CSR) in the Dioceses of Canterbury and Rochester, which has the advantage of treating the economy as integral to a wide range of social issues, but which puts tremendous pressure on a small CSR staff.

A further means by which this might be done was outlined in *Local Economy-based Industrial Mission* (14), in which the need for careful analysis of, and reflection on, the local economy, would lead to a setting of priorities, appropriate action and review. For such a development of responsibility for mission in the local economy to be achieved, with its consequent re-ordering of ministerial responsibilities, considerable training of parish clergy and continuing professional support will be necessary. This clearly implies that the services of one or more properly trained Mission staff in each District or Region will still be required, and perhaps the setting up of an appropriate regional training scheme from which clergy and at least some lay people could benefit. The churches in a town or area would need a 'Faith and Work' Group as one of the main ways in which Christian men and women who could be active in their work communities could be trained and supported. This work of the churches to play their proper role in the local economy would also need to be adequately resourced.

As churches in a District or Region develop their Mission in the Local Economy they will usually appoint one of the members as their representative to key bodies. The experience of IM staff as representatives of the churches in industry, together with the theology they used and skills they developed (see Chapter 5) will be of use to them. It is also worth pointing out that IM from the earliest days found it had to act ecumenically, and needed ecumenical bodies to underwrite the breadth of their representation.

In recent years it has been found helpful for ministering effectively in an multi-faith setting, for the chaplain to have an explicit agreement with a group such as the local Interfaith Council or Forum, in which the chaplain agrees to refer people (with their permission) to the appropriate representative of their own faith for further contact. In other areas of life in which chaplaincy has been provided (hospitals, prisons, universities, the military) efforts to build multi-faith chaplaincy teams are beginning to take place, and this is developing in at least one industrial mission project. (15) The possibilities of doing theological thinking in a multi-faith context were well illustrated by a seminar called 'Ethics in a Global Economy' held in London in 2008 and sponsored by 'Faiths in London's Economy'. (16)

Partnerships with relevant bodies inside and outside the churches are, therefore, both practically and theologically necessary. They greatly increase the influence of the churches and make their work better informed and more effective. They give the church representatives, ordained or lay, valuable opportunities to identify God at work in the lives and work of others, to point this out in appropriate ways, and to encourage greater awareness of God's concerns.

Much of this representative work will fall to ordained ministers, some in stipendiary posts, and others through their own employment. If their initial and in-service training fails to give them a theology of God's action in the world they may find it hard to see a valid ministry beyond the fringe of the church. The distortion of 'Mission-shaped Church' into 'Church-shaped mission' is a likely outcome. As described in Chapter 6, Industrial Mission has had a remarkable record in the training of ordinands and junior clergy – the two authors of this study first met on a course for ordinands run by Scunthorpe Industrial Mission in 1966. Such courses, usually set in industrial environments, both provided valuable shop-floor experience for participants and grounded their theological and pastoral studies for ministry in the broader realities of the economy and human behaviour within it. Wickham's original proposal for longer-term industrial and residential experience of ordinands in working-class communities in Sheffield was of immense benefit to several hundred young clergy. It repeated Ian Fraser's recommendation at the end of his six months' experience of working in a Fife paper mill in 1942-43. It is now widely recognised that the training of future Christian ministers needs to include some urban experience and, where their college is in a rural or small town setting, an urban placement. For those entering ministerial training in mid-life after a career in secular employment such placements will not be as important as the acquisition of skills to reflect upon their prior experience so as to integrate their theological studies with their previous experience of work.

It is inevitable that with the withdrawal of resources in recent years, industrial mission teams now find it very difficult to provide any structured courses or modules of ministerial training. However, experienced IM practitioners are still able to help equip new ministers with the theological, pastoral, social and economic insights they need to carry forward mission now. (See also the Appendix to Chapter 4, *Core Skills for Workplace Chaplains.*)

So what is the living legacy of IM?

We hope that we have sufficiently described the ways in which the experience of IM in the twentieth century in what at first seemed the alien world of heavy industry can and should be employed by the British churches as they carry out their mission in the twenty-first century. We have identified the key features of IM which helped it to operate with a degree of acknowledgement and goodwill from both society at large and from the churches. 'Success' is of course something different, given the hope and the vision of transformation through Christ which many in Industrial Mission shared and still share. We believe that this model of mission provides a basis for an appropriate mission for modern Britain in the early twenty-first century. Given the grace of God, it will be the source of far more creative Christian thinking in the future.

In all these and other ways we hope the British churches can maintain a persistent and informed Christian presence within all the diverse communities and groups of contemporary British society. The purpose of this presence will be to keep alive 'the rumour of God' for everyone, and thus to allow everyone the opportunity to respond to God's love and truth for themselves, and for the economy, the communities and the world of which they are part. In this way the task of mission will be continued, the task of transforming people and structures, and so in very practical ways to build the Kingdom of God in our world.

With this great vision still before us, it might be as well to end with a reflection which was attributed to Archbishop Oscar Romero, who was murdered in El Salvador for opposing a brutal government there, but which was actually written by John Dearden, Cardinal Archbishop of Boston:

It helps now and then to take a step back and take the long view.
The Kingdom is not only beyond our efforts, it is even
beyond our vision.
We accomplish in our lifetime only a tiny fraction of the
magnificent enterprise that is
God's work.
Nothing we do is complete, which is another way of saying
that the Kingdom always lies
beyond us.

No statement says all that can be said.
No prayer fully expresses our faith.
No confession brings perfection, no pastoral visit brings
wholeness.
No programme accomplishes the Church's mission.
No set of goals and objectives include everything.

We plant the seed that one day will grow.
We water seeds already planted knowing that they hold
future promise.
We lay foundations that will need further development.
We provide yeast that produces effects far beyond our
capabilities.

We cannot do everything and there is a sense of liberation
in realising this.
This enables us to do something, and to do it very well.
It may be incomplete but it is a beginning, a step along the
way, an opportunity
for the Lord's grace to enter and do the rest.
We may never see the end results, but that is the difference
between the
master builder and the workers.
We are workers, not master builders, ministers not Messiahs.
We are the prophets of a future not our own.

Notes and references to this chapter

1. Quoted in Michael Atkinson, *Theological Influences in the Early Years of Industrial Mission,* p 8, essay in *Thinking in Practice,* Working Papers from Industrial Mission 3, IMA Theological Development Group (1981).

2. National Centre for Social Research 26th Annual Report, January 2010, quoted in *The Guardian,* 4 March 2011.

3. E R Wickham, *Church and People in an Industrial City,* Lutterworth (1957) p 230.

4. See (a) *Poverty, Debt and the Financial Crisis,* papers for a conference organised by Churches Together in Britain and Ireland 'to reflect theologically on the root causes of the present economic crisis and the response of the church in terms of its prophetic, pastoral and partnership roles and responsibilities'; see www.ctbi.org.uk/resources and also (b)*Crisis and Recovery: Ethics, Economics and Justice,* ed. Rowan Williams and Larry Elliott (2010).

5. A full list can be found in the Bibliography. A valuable summary of this work is in *The Church and Economic Life; a documentary study 1945 to the present* by Malcolm Brown and Paul Ballard, Epworth (2006).

6. For a statement of all the Foundation's current activities, please visit www.wtf.org.uk A good example of the Foundation's work in supporting the churches' engagement with economic life is: Malcolm Brown and Robin Morrison, *Church, Change and the Economy,* William Temple Foundation (1999).

7. David J Bosch, *Transforming Mission,* Orbis Books (1991) p 452.

8. *Mission-shaped Church,* Church House Publishing (2004) p 91.

9. Philip Bloy, *The Call to Mission Answered; Ted Wickham and the Sheffield Industrial Mission* (2000) p 10.

10. *Theology and Politics,* IMA Theology Development Group.

11. Further titles in *Working Papers from Industrial Mission* can be found in the Bibliography.

12. *Theology and Politics,* p iii.

13. Malcolm Brown and Robin Morrison, *Church, Change and the Economy,* William Temple Foundation (1999).

14. Mostyn Davies, Roger Clarke, Bernard Brown and Ray Taylor (authors), *Local Economy-based Industrial Mission.*
15. Greenwich Peninsula Multi-Faith Chaplaincy, led by Revd Dr Malcolm Torry.
16 For a report on this event by Jonathan Evens, see *Faith in Business*, Vol.12, No.3 (2009).

BIBLIOGRAPHY

The John Rylands Library, Manchester, holds the IMA's collection of books and papers including copies of all the *Newsletters* and *IMAgendas* referenced in this book. The catalogue can be searched at:-www.industrialmissionhistory.org.uk Permission to visit the collection should be sought from the IMA Secretary.

12 Key works on Industrial Mission in the UK

Bagshaw, Paul; *The Church beyond the Church – Sheffield Industrial Mission 1944 – 1994*; Sheffield, Industrial Mission in South Yorkshire (1994) 144 pp.
A thorough history of IM's most influential project which does not avoid the theological and ecclesiastical problems faced.

Bloy, Philip; *The Call to Mission answered, Ted Wickham and the Sheffield Industrial Mission 1944 – 1959*; Northampton, Disciples Press (2000) 140 pp.
Philip Bloy was a member of the Sheffield team in the 1950s, and spent the rest of his ministry in IM. A unique personal account of the Mission in its earliest days.

Matsumoto, Shigeko; *A Critique of British Industrial Mission as a response of the Church in Modern Industrial Society*; A brief summary of her M A thesis published by GS BSR Industrial Affairs Committee IC/11/85 (1985) 36 pp.
An exploration of the sociological and theological gaps between church and world, with some analysis of the inability of IM to influence the church's understanding of Mission.

Reindorp, Julian; *Equipping Christians at Work*; London, Industrial Christian Fellowship (2000) 99 pp. A useful summary of the history and theology of IM with the application of that experience to the life of the local church.

Rogerson, John (editor) *Industrial Mission in a Changing world; papers from the Jubilee Conference of the Sheffield Industrial Mission*; Sheffield, Sheffield Academic Press (1996) 192 pp.
18 Conference papers, 11 by IM staff on aspects of the theology and practice of IM.

Ross, Donald M; *God it's Monday, Some reflections on the History of Industrial Mission*; Edinburgh, St Andrew Press (1997) 141 pp.
IM in Scotland followed a similar path to that in England, but working with a different relationship between the Established Church and society. Donald Ross was a leading figure in IM in Scotland, first in Glasgow and then as National Organiser.

Taylor, Richard; *Christians in an Industrial Society;* London, SCM Press (1961) 128 pp.
An early overview of IM in six cities and lay movements within the churches.

Torry, Malcolm; *Bridgebuilders, Workplace Chaplaincy – a History;* Norwich,; Canterbury Press (2010) 205 pp.
A thorough history of IM work particularly in Sheffield and South London but largely omitting IM projects outside of workplaces and within the churches.

Brown, Malcolm and Ballard, Paul; *The Church and Economic Life, a documentary study 1945 to the present*; Peterborough; Epworth (2006).
A collection of documents by the churches on economic and industrial issues, together with excellent introductory articles.

Phipps, Simon; *God on Monday;* London, Hodder and Stoughton (1966).
After working in IM in Coventry Simon Phipps went on to become Bishop of Lincoln and Chair of the Church of England Industrial Committee. This book reflects on his time in Coventry, and contains much valuable theological analysis of the basis of Christian mission.

Wickham, E R (Ted*); Church and People in an Industrial City*; London, Lutterworth (1957) 292 pp.

A careful study of the church's failure to respond to the industrial revolution in Britain's archetypal industrial city. It concludes with a chapter in which he sketches the theology and organisation necessary for 'the mission of the church in an industrial society'.

Wilkie, George; *Christian thinking about Industrial life;* Edinburgh, St Andrew Press (1980) 78 pp
A brief but perceptive introduction to the whole subject of the relation of Christian living to industrial life by a very experienced industrial chaplain.

Papers published by the William Temple Foundation, Manchester

Kane, Margaret; *Theological Development – an Experiment in the North East* (1980).

Cordingley, Brian; *USA and El Salvador Sketches;* Occasional Papers No 18 (1990).

Brown, Malcolm and Morrison, Robin; *Church Change and Economy – How can the Churches engage with today's economy?* (1999).

Papers produced by the Theology Development Group of the IMA

Working Papers from Industrial Mission; lithographed; A5 booklets.

ONE Theology and Politics (1978).

TWO The End of Work – papers on Theology and Technological Change (1980).

THREE Thinking in Practice: Theology and Industrial Mission (1980).

FOUR Spirituality and Necessity (1982).

FIVE Changing Industrial Mission – models and hopes (1983).

Davies, Mostyn; *Industrial Mission – the Anatomy of a Crisis* (1991).

The Church of England;
usually published in London by the Church Information Office (CIO). Some can be accessed via www.cofe.anglican.org/documents.

The Task of the Church in Relation to Industry (1959).

Redundancy (1962).

Work in Britain today (1969).

Wickham, E R; *Growth and Inflation* (1975).

Gilbertson. Geoffrey; *Power Sharing in Industry* (1975).

Adams, Kenneth; *Ethical Choice and Business Responsibilities* (1975).

Edwards, David L; *The State of the Nation; A Christian Approach to Britain's Economic Crisis* (1976).

Understanding Closed Shops – a Christian enquiry into compulsory trade union membership (1976) GS (Misc) 66.

Work and the Future – Technology, World development and Jobs in the Eighties (1979) GS 429.

Winters of Discontent – Industrial Conflict a Christian perspective (1981) GS 481.

Transnational Corporations Confronting the Issues (1983).

Perspectives on Economics (1984).

Growth, Justice and Work (1985).

All that is unseen; a new look at women and work (1986).

Muir, Kevin; *Industrial Mission – Catholic style* (1987).

The Ethics of Acquisition (1989).

A Series on *Industrial Mission and the Church in Britain Today:-*

Sedgwick, Peter; *Not Ceasing from Exploring* (1987).

Beales, Chris; *Tools for Fools, parts One and Two* (1987).

The Church and the Miners' Strike (1986).

Industrial Mission – an Appraisal, the Church's Response to the Changing Industrial and Economic Order (1988).

Dear Mr Green – responses to Industrial Mission – an Appraisal (1989).

Church and Economy – Effective Industrial Mission for the 1990s (1989) GS 886.

Ministry and Mission Examined, Stories and Reflections on Industrial Mission Today (1989).

For the Board for Mission and Unity:-

Today's Missionaries (1973) GS 153.

The Measure of Mission (1987).

For the Board of Education:-

Called to New Life, the World of Lay Discipleship (1999) GS (Misc) 546.

Faith in the City, The Report of the Archbishop's Commission on Urban Life and Faith, London (1985).

Mission-shaped Church, a report of a working group of the Church of England's Mission and Public Affairs Council (2004).

British Council of Churches

The Church and Industry – an assessment of the need and the Response so far made; Suggestions for advance (1958).

The Churches Consortium on Industrial Mission (CCIM)
Formed in 1975 by the British Council of Churches.

Guidelines on the Task, Organisation, Appointments and Continuity of Industrial Mission (1977).

Appointments to IM – towards a general pattern (1979).

A Survey on Teamwork – recommended paper Three (1981).

Starting the Work – a Basic Manual for Industrial Chaplains recommended paper Five (1982).

The Churches commitment to work in Industry (1982).

After the Council of Churches for Britain and Ireland was formed in 1990, and the number of national staff dealing with economic and industrial issues drastically reduced, CCIM was replaced by INDEM, which operates largely as an electronic network sharing common issues and interests between national denominational officers and those engaged in workplace chaplaincy and faith-work projects.

Churches Together in Britain and Ireland

Unemployment and the Future of Work – an Enquiry for the Churches (1997).

Barrow, Simon and Smith, Graeme (editors) *Christian Mission in Western Society,* London (2001).

General Bibliography

A New Dictionary of Christian Ethics; articles on Labour Movements Trade Unions by Ronald Preston, London, SCM Press (1986).

Alinsky, Saul; *Rules for Radicals;* New York, Random House (1971).

Ballard, Paul and Pritchard, John; *Practical Theology in Action;,* London, SPCK (1996).

Baxter, Jim; *Inside Industry – the History of the South Australian Inter-Church Trade and Industry Mission*; Adelaide, Inter-Church Trade and Industry Mission (1985).

Berger, Peter; *A Rumor of Angels;* New York, Anchor at Random House (1970).

Bevans, Stephen B; *Models of Contextual Theology*; New York, Orbis (1997).

Bonhoeffer, Dietrich; edited by Eberhard Bethge *Letters and Papers from Prison;* London, SCM Press (1971).

Borrowdale, Anne; *A Woman's Work – Changing Christian Attitudes*; London, SPCK (1989).

Bosanquet, Mary; *The Life and Death of Dietrich Bonhoeffer*, London, Hodder & Stoughton (1968).

Bosch, David; *Transforming Mission, Paradigm shifts in Theology of Mission*; New York, Orbis (1996).

Breaking Barriers Nairobi 1975; edited by D M Paton; London, SPCK for the World Council of Churches (1976).

Bultmann, Rudolph; *New Testament and Mythology and other Basic Writings;* New York, Fortress Press (1984).

Catherwood, H F R; *The Christian in Industrial Society*; London, Tyndale Press (1964).

Changing Europe – changing urban, industrial and rural mission; Manchester, ECG (1992).

Christianity and Industrial Problems; The Report of the Archbishop's Fifth Commission (1918) quoted in S G Evans; *The Social Hope of the Christian Church;* London, Hodder and Stoughton (1965).

Claringbull, Dennis; *Front line Mission, Ministry in the Market Place*; Norwich, Canterbury Press (1994).

Cooper, Trevor; *Who goes there? A challenge to humanity;* Milton Keynes, Authorhouse (2009).

Cope, Peter and Gilbert, Christine; *The Incredible Flying Machine – a way of making Christian decisions*; Black Country Urban and Industrial Mission (1992) later published as an Audenshaw Paper.

Cordingley, Brian; *Sketches of Urban Industrial Mission in Some European Countries*; Manchester, European Contact Group on Church and Industry (1973).

Cox, Harvey; *The Secular City;* London, SCM Press (1966).

Cuttell, Colin; *Ministry without Portfolio*; London, Toc H (1962).

Erelander, Lillemore; *Faith in the World of Work – on the theology of work as lived by the French Worker-Priests and British Industrial Mission*; Uppsala, University of Uppsala (1991).

Fox, Alan; *Industrial Sociology and Industrial Relations*; London, Donovan Commission Research Paper No 3, HMSO (1966).

Fraser, Ian M; *Re-inventing Theology as the People's Work*; Glasgow, Wild Goose; revised edition (1988).

Fuller, John and Vaughan, Patrick; (editors) *Working for the Kingdom, the story of Ministers in Secular Employment*; London, SPCK (1986) see the article by Eric Forshaw.

Gowland D and Roebuck S; *Never call retreat – a biography of Bill Gowland;* London, Chester House Publications (1990).

Goyder, George; *The Just Enterprise*; London, Andre Deutsch (1987).

Graham, Elaine and Halsey, Margaret; *Life cycles; Women and Pastoral Care*; London, SPCK (1993).

Green, Laurie; *Let's Do Theology – a Pastoral Cycle Resource Book;* London, Mowbrays (1990).

Grundy, Malcolm; *An Unholy Conspiracy*; London, Canterbury Press (1992).

Hewitt, Gordon (editor) *Strategist for the Spirit, Leslie Hunter Bishop of Sheffield 1939 – 1962*; Oxford, Beckett (1985).

Industrial Democracy: ways forward in Britain and West Germany; Anglo- German Foundation for the Study of Industrial Society (1979).

Iremonger F A, *William Temple – Archbishop of Canterbury;* Oxford, Oxford University Press (1948).

Kane, Margaret; *Gospel in an Industrial Society*; SCM Press (1980).

Kane, Margaret; *Theology in an Industrial Society*; SCM Press (1975)

Kane, Margaret; *What kind of God? Reflections on working with People and Churches in North-East England;* London, SCM Press (1968).

Lewin,Hugh (compiler) *A Community of Clowns – Testimonies of People in Urban Rural Mission;* Geneva, World Council of Churches (1987).

Mantle, John; *Britain's First Worker-Priests*; London, SCM Press (2000).

Multinational Companies – a working document; European Contact Group on Church and Industry (1976).

Niebuhr, H Richard; *Christ and Culture;* Torchbooks (1951).

Niebuhr, Reinhold; *Moral Man and Immoral Society;* London, SCM Press (1963).

Northcott, Michael; *The Church and Secularisation: Urban Industrial Mission in North-East England;* Bern, Peter Lang (1989).

Ormiston, Hugh and Ross, Donald M (editors) *New Patterns of Work*; Edinburgh, St Andrews Press (1990).

Platten, S (editor) *Runcie: on Reflection;* Norwich, Canterbury Press (2002).

Redundancy – the Last Option; Newport and Gwent Industrial Mission (1979).

Redundant? A personal survival kit; Newport and Gwent Industrial Mission (1975).

Report of the Sixth Assembly of the World Council of Churches in Vancouver; SPCK for the WCC (1984).

Robinson J; *Honest to God;* London, SCM Press (1963).

Siefer, Gregor; *The Church and Industrial Society, complete history of the Worker-Priests – and the present dilemma*; London, Darton Longman Todd (1964).

Strategies for Engaging with Working Life; Prague, ECG (2000).

Symanowski, Horst; *The Christian Witness in an Industrial Society*; London, Collins (1966).

Tate, Jane; *Penny a Bag;* Leeds, Yorkshire and Humberside Low Pay Unit (1990).

Temple, William; *Christianity and Social Order*, Harmondsworth, Penguin (1942).

Templeton, Elizabeth (editor) *A Woman's Place...? Women and Work;* Edinburgh, St Andrews Press (1993) Articles by M Halsey, A Borrowdale and D Leppington.

The Report of the Royal Commission on Trade Unions and Employers Associations chaired by Lord Donovan; London, HMSO (1968).

Tillich, Paul; *Systematic Theology I*, quoted by E J Tinsley in *Paul Tillich*; London Epworth Press (1973).

Tillich, Paul; *The Shaking of the Foundations;* London, Penguin (1962).

Transnational Corporations – a Challenge for Christians and Churches; Geneva, World Council of Churches Commission on Participation in Development (1982)

Tonkinson, David; *Recognising sixty years plus – views of IM;* Microsoft Word and PDF on CD-ROM.

Urban Industrial Mission in European Countries; ECG (1979).

Urban Rural Mission Reflections; Geneva, World Council of Churches (1986).

Velten, Georges; *Mission in Industrial France*; London, SCM Press (1968).

Wickham, E R; *Encounter with Modern Society;* London, Lutterworth (1964).

INDEX

Airports 19, 86, 91, 145
Ambulance Service 86
Apprentice training 94, 110
Archbishop's Commission on
   Christianity and Industrial
   Problems 3, 137
Asda 85
Atkinson, Michael 6, 69
Atherton, John 69, 142
Attwood, Tony 96, 98
Auckland, Clifford 97
Australia 90

Bagshaw, Paul 7, 36, 40
Ballard, Paul 46, 52
Bardsley, Cuthbert 2, 78, 82, 87
Baynes, Tim 79
Beales, Chris 127
Beattie, Noel 22, 83, 84
Berger, Peter 47
Beveridge, W (Bill) 94
Birmingham 3ff
Black Country 55, 143
Bloy, Philip 6, 30, 35ff, 141
Bluewater centre 22
Bonhoeffer, Dietrich 42, 43
Bristol 4ff, 10, 63, 97, 128
British Council of Churches
   (BCC) 8, 34, 119
British Rail (BR) 10
British Steel Corporation
   (BSC)'10, 69, 96, 97, 109
Brown, Malcolm 53
Bultmann, Rudolf 40ff

CAFOD 120, 121
Cambridge 54, 84, 85, 93, 131
Central Electricity Generating
   Board (CEGB) 14, 110
Challen, Peter 7
Chambers of Commerce 105
Christian Aid 120, 121
Christian Frontier Council 31
Christian Newsletter 31, 32, 34
Christian Social Union 2, 30
Christians at Work groups 128
Christmas, Alan 132
Church Commissioners 10, 20,
   118, 120
Church of England Board for
   Social Responsibility 13, 14,
   16ff, 118, 119, 141
Church of England General
   Synod 5, 13, 17, 18, 121,
   126, 129,
Church of England Industrial
   and Economic Affairs
   Committee 20
Church of England; Church
   Assembly 5
Church of Scotland 2, 32
Church Urban Fund 21, 106
Churches Consortium on
   Industrial Mission (CCIM), 9,
   12, 15, 21, 25, 64, 137
Churches together in Britain
   and Ireland (CCBI) 22, 122,
   146
Claringbull, Denis 87

Clemitson, Ivor 7, 118
Coal Industry 14, 19, 21, 64, 82, 98, 146
Conference on Christian Politics, Economics and Citizenship (COPEC) 3, 30
Congregational Church 6, 126, 130
Cooper, Trevor 15, 115ff
Cope, Peter 55, 143
Cordingley, Brian 79, 118
Core Skills for Workplace Chaplains 24, 58, 89, 102, 150
Corporate Social Responsibility 119ff
Coventry 5, 6, 15, 22, 91, 115ff
Cox, Harvey 53
Crawley 6
Croydon 7, 87
Cuttell, Colin 2, 78, 79
Czock, Horst 115

Dalling, Antony 15, 21, 61
Davies, Mostyn 11, 17
Deductive methods 46, 55ff
Department of Employment 10, 63
Doing Theology 9, 52, 63, 65, 131ff, 141, 142
Dudman, W (Bill) 7
Duncan, Peter 112

Eagle, Julian 13, 118ff
East London 5, 70, 112
Ecumenical Council for Corporate Responsibility (ECCR) 121ff
El Salvador 118, 151
Emergency Services 86, 145
Employers Associations 9, 105
Equal opportunities 64, 106

Erlander, Lillemor 22
European Contact Group (ECG) 11, 16, 61, 62, 105ff, 111, 113, 114, 120
European Economic Community 13, 119,
European Union 106
Evangelism 5, 20, 21, 32, 36, 37, 58, 79, 102, 133, 135

Faith in the City 13, 21, 137
Fire and Rescue Service 21, 86, 110
Firth Vickers 34, 78, 82
Fraser, Ian 2, 14, 32, 33, 49ff, 139, 149

General Motors 11, 62, 112, 114
German Democratic Republic (DDR) 115ff
Gilbert, Christine 55
Girls Friendly Society 105
Gowland, W (Bill) 4
Green, Laurie 52
Grimsby 13
Grundy, Malcolm 77
Gutknecht, Max 112ff

Halsey, Margaret 80
Hammersley, John 85
Hancock, Kay 4
Hardwick, Graham 90
Hayes, Barbara 122
Hayes, Leslie 3
Hayler, Peter 84, 93
Hermeneutic/Pastoral Cycle 52
Hertfordshire and Bedfordshire 11, 51, 61, 62, 129, 132
Homeworkers 105ff
Hunter, Leslie 1, 3, 7, 29, 31, 32, 34, 82, 130, 135, 141

ICI 121
IMAgenda 23, 24, 65
INDEM 21
Independence (of a Chaplain)
65, 86, 90ff, 97
Induction Course 8, 14, 15, 24,
52, 65, 89
Inductive methods 9, 46ff, 55,
133, 139
Industrial Christian Fellowship
(ICF) 2, 30, 141
Industrial disputes 95ff
Industrial Mission an Appraisal
17ff, 64, 66, 135
Industrial Mission Association
(IMA)
6, 8, 9, 10, 13ff, 20, 23, 24, 52,
58, 64, 89, 96, 102, 110,
119, 131
Industrial Mission in South
Yorkshire - see Sheffield
Industrial Mission
IMA National Conference 48,
65, 120
Industrial relations 9, 10, 47,
51, 61, 89, 96, 127, 136

Jackson, Michael 6ff, 43
Jamieson, Lyn 65
Jenkins, David 48, 49, 139
Jenkins, Maurice 4
Jones, Martin 22

Kane, Margaret 4, 48, 69
Kendal, Stephen 96
Kent 15, 22
Keymen 79
Kierkegaard, Soren 33
Kingdom of God 31, 37, 39,
47, 53, 92, 138ff, 150
Kirchliche Dienst in Arbeitswelt
(KDA) 115
Kodak 61

Lay groups 8, 126, 127, 143
Lay people 29, 35, 51, 55, 64,
70, 79, 126, 128, 142ff, 148
Leeds 22, 105ff
Leppington, Dian 105
Lincoln 10, 22, 84
Liverpool 5, 16, 22
Local Authorities 10, 86, 107,
137
London North of the Thames
(see also East London and
South London) 19, 20, 61,
70, 94, 109, 121, 129
Lucas Aerospace 13, 49
Lurkings, E (Ted) 16
Luton 4, 7, 22, 112ff, 132

Manchester 5, 11, 14, 59, 64,
70, 79, 91, 109, 128
Manpower Services
Commission (MSC) 10, 13,
15, 110
Matsumoto, Shigeko 16, 125
Maurice, Frederick Denison
29, 31
Methodist Church 4, 20, 126
Metro centre 21, 85
Milton Keynes 128
Miners' Strike 14, 96
Ministerial Training 5, 7, 18,
130ff, 143, 145, 150
Moll, Randall 129
Morris, Anne 64
Multinationals (MNC) – see
Transnational Corporations

National Industrial Mission 10,
13, 14, 107ff, 110ff, 146
National Union of Mineworkers
14, 98
Navvy Mission 1, 2, 30
Newell, Roy 118

Newport and Gwent 10, 62
Niebuhr, Reinhold 40, 43
Niebuhr, Richard 47
Nind, Bob 120
Norfolk and Waveney 127
Norris, Alison 16
Northampton 7, 83

Oldham, J H (Joe) 30, 31, 34, 65
Opel 11, 62, 112ff
Oxford 122, 132

Pastoral Studies 131ff, 149
Paxton, John 20
Percy, Chris 13
Peterborough 59, 127
Phipps, Simon 6
Plant Closures 52, 96ff
Police Service 21, 86, 110, 144
Port Talbot 6
Portsmouth 121
Potter, John 97
Preston, Ronald 40, 61
Pritchard, John 46, 52

QinetiQ 91, 93

Racial justice 12, 13, 65, 120
Ragg, John 4
Ramsey, Michael 9, 48
Reading 5
Redundancy 10, 59, 62ff, 96, 98
Reindorp, Julian 128, 143
Retail chaplaincy 19, 21, 85, 86, 145
Robinson, John 43
Rochester 5, 6, 148
Rogan, John 6, 70
Roman Catholic Church 9, 60
Ross, Donald 133

Scuffham, Frank 59
Scunthorpe 6, 149
Sheffield, City 32, 135
Sheffield Industrial Mission 1, 3ff, 11, 22, 23, 33, 35ff, 39ff, 43, 78, 80, 93, 96, 97 109, 125, 130, 131, 149
Siemens.2, 78, 82
Singh, Ray 65
Smith, Olwen 64
Snap-break meetings 78, 93
South Africa 13, 118ff
South Hampshire 22, 121
South London 15
South London Industrial Mission 2, 6, 54, 65, 78, 79, 109, 121
South Yorkshire 15, 96, 98
Southampton 13, 118, 119
Springe, Christa 16
Steel Chaplains 10, 96
Stevens, Ralph 4
Stockton 6
Stubbs, Ian 16
Studdert-Kennedy, Geoffrey 30
Sunderland, Chris 128
Surrey and North-east Hampshire 91
Swynnerton; Royal Ordnance Factory 2, 33

Tawney, Richard 30, 65
Taylor, Richard 6
Teesside 7, 10, 107, 118, 128
Telford 85, 143
Temple; William 30, 31, 65
Thatcher, Margaret 12, 18, 19, 83
Theological Colleges 9, 11, 14, 51, 130ff
Theological Grid 52ff
Theology Development Group (TDG) 13ff, 23, 65ff, 69, 142

Tillich, Paul 38ff, 43
Torry, Malcolm 2, 78
Trades unions 4, 6, 8, 9, 10,
    13, 19, 22, 47, 50, 59ff, 105,
    109, 112, 116, 118
Transnational corporations 61,
    112ff, 114, 120
Transport and General Workers
    Union (TGWU) 13, 119

Unemployed People 10, 13,
    15, 17, 22, 63, 69, 110
Unemployment 10, 13, 15, 21,
    38, 62, 65, 87, 98, 110, 131,
    137
Unemployment and the Future
    of Work 21
United Reformed Church 126,
    130

Vauxhall 11, 62, 112ff

Ward, Rodney 69
Wardman, Carol 128
Warner, Chris 23

Warrington 6
Welbourn, David 13. 91
West, Mike 52, 53, 112ff
White, Crispin 119ff
Wickham, E R (Ted) 1ff, 5, 7, 8,
    10, 23, 29, 33ff, 78, 82, 107,
    125, 130, 136, 141
William Temple College 35, 47
William Temple Foundation 8,
    14, 65, 141
Wilson, Keith 23
Working Papers from Industrial
    Mission 69
Works' Padres 34, 87
World Council of Churches
    (WCC) 13, 17, 19, 31, 49,
    61, 120
WCC-Urban Rural Mission
    committee (WCC-URM) 16,
    111
World faiths 136, 137, 147
Wright, W (Bill) 6, 10

York 20
Youth Training Scheme 15